Guilt – Right or Wrong! Who Decides? We Decide!

Author: Shivi Goyal

Guilt – Right or Wrong?

Dedicated to GodSend

You came my way when I was surrounded with darkness. You became my shining light in the armour. You abetted me with the real meaning of our karmic deeds and detached life from all the evils, wherein I explored my inner being to the fullest. Still the quest is on. You unexpectedly came into my life and with your warmth I'm touched deep. With you I know that GOD exists in the form of you.

"To think of you is to smile and shine bright."

My Gratitude!

Guilt – Right or Wrong?

Contents

Prologue	08
Acknowledgement	14
The Real Truth About Guilt	19
Facts About Guilt	21
Good Guilt	25
Bad Guilt	29
Survivor Guilt – The Epic	32
Art Of Guilt	33
The Rational Approach To Guilt	39
Types Of Guilt	41
Neurotic Guilt	43
Toxic or Free-Floating Guilt	46
Drowning Under Bestie's Guilt	50

Guilt – Right or Wrong?

Natural Guilt	*58*
Feeling Regretful - A Barrier In Self-Growth	*61*
Existential Guilt	*67*
Effects Of Guilt	*70*
Dealing With Guilt	*72*
Wipe It Out - Wipe The Slate Clean	*76*
Estranged Within – Estranged Guilt	*78*
Bitter Sweet Sour	*86*
An Apology To My Future Self	*94*
New Baby – New Life	*98*
Resilience Is The Antidote To Guilt In Teens	*101*
Heal yourself – Test yourself	*110*
Assess Your Guilt Quotient	*114*
Talk To Yourself	*123*
Assess Your Guilt Proneness Scale	*146*
Journal Prompt For Manifestation	*158*

Journal Prompts For Vivid Moods	*173*
Author's Suggestions To Reconcile Your Guilt	*186*
Heal Your Inner Being! (Journal Prompt)	*189*
About Author	*190*
Books By Author	*192*
Citations	*193*

Prologue

About the author

I met Shivi Goyal through writing, both of us travel bloggers who loved nothing more than telling a good story about our travel adventures and I quickly learned that not only is she a travel blogger, but she is a life coach, YouTuber, digital marketer, artist, entrepreneur, humanitarian, a proud single mom and of course an amazing HUMAN BEING!

At the time I met her, Shivi was already a Guinness Book of World Records holder, an award-winning author of two individual published books and had published over 6 anthologies! She is compassionate about her writings and has a vision of healing people with consciousness and mindfulness. So I was thrilled and honoured when she asked me to write a foreword for her newly published book Guilt – Right or Wrong? Who decides? We decide!

About the book

It's not what happens to us, but our response to what happens to us that hurts us. Between the stimulus of actions and reactions, we often tend to get guilt in our lives. Here it is prudent that we create a vibration full of understanding and consciousness that will help us to get over our guilt in our lives, for others and for us. This book will help to break this chain.

In the book, Ms Goyal demonstrates that the problem we face is when we get conditioned by our minds and thoughts. We face trouble rising from within us. All the negative emotions are our reactions to the external factors, which lead us to further devastating emotions like guilt, shame and embarrassment. This can be avoided, and if at all it occurs there are ways to heal and practice self-healing.

This book will take you on a journey of real-life experiences which will, in turn, support you to get over your guilt.

Definitely one of the best readings on the subject of guilt and how to overcome it. The author does not just tell you to get over it but she shows you how to. This is a book you can go back to time and again. Highly recommended.

Thola Bennie

(Author "Fit and Fabulous at 50 (KDP)"

Phoenix Rising Life Coach & Podcaster)

∞∞∞∞∞∞∞∞∞∞∞∞∞∞∞∞∞∞∞∞∞∞∞∞∞∞∞∞∞∞∞∞∞∞∞∞∞

A chance meeting on LinkedIn and few moons, lead to our knowing each other as professionals followed by individuals. Shivi is a strong-headed woman who has her life quiver full of powerful and enchanting words and responses. Her inquisitive nature digs deep into the human subconscious mind emerging out with ways still unknown.

Guilt-Right or Wrong? Who Decides? We Decide, is one such path-breaking self-help read that dwells into this generally considered negative emotion "guilt". Shivi explores how guilt carries an unrecognized positive side that guides us to reach up to righteous decisions. She jots down practical ways of doing so with a touch of striking relatability.

Shivi advocates changing the belief systems that can help us create a path for our guilt-free future.

I strongly recommend and wish unlimited readings and reaching outs of her latest book Guilt-Right or Wrong? Who Decides? We Decide.

Sending in zillions of wishes to my award-winning, Guinness Book of World Record holder pal for her undying passion for words and the world. Happy Readings.

Rj Pinky

Station Head and Mentor, Lakecity Voice Digital Campus Radio. Ad Director, Voice over Artist, Show Host.

There's so much out there to explore and experience. That's what life is about and Shivi has done a great job here. Through her book, I somehow felt that I could too, live the most fulfilling, epic life possible. With no regrets!

Kudos to you Shivi for penning it down so gracefully.

Vaibhav Bhargava

(Food & Beverage Consultant) Director Abv Hospitalities private limited

∞∞∞∞∞∞∞∞∞∞∞∞∞∞∞∞∞∞∞∞∞∞∞∞∞∞∞∞∞∞∞∞∞

I was delighted when I received a request from Shivi Goyal to write a short foreword for her upcoming Self Help book. I have always been a fan of Shivi Goyal's work for her writings are raw and relatedly true. I look up to her not only for her work but also for what she is. She radiates so much positivity. Her previous books on women empowerment are a must-read. In her upcoming self-help book, Shivi Goyal talks about appreciating life and complaining less. I am sure this book will serve as a source of self-improvement for all.

Guilt – Right or Wrong?

Looking forward to reading many more from her and wishing her all the best.

Ekta Murarka

Book & Beauty Blogger

∞∞∞∞∞∞∞∞∞∞∞∞∞∞∞∞∞∞∞∞∞∞∞∞∞∞∞∞∞∞∞∞

Acknowledgement

"To give thanks in solitude is enough. Thanksgiving has wings and goes where it must go. Your prayer knows much more about it than you do."

Victor Hugo

I always get sweaty-palm edgy when I'm writing my acknowledgements for my latest book. I'm terrified that I will miss out someone who needs to be thanked, then enormously overcompensate when I see them again in person and give them an awkward sweaty hug. I don't want it to happen, thus slow motion claps for all who have helped me in my journey in whatever I'm today.

First and foremost, humble and respectful thank to My Mother, she is cute, adoring, understanding in whatever I do and massively supporting.

A huge round of applause for my proof-readers, editor, publisher, and beta readers. Beta readers are like

Grammarsaurus Rex* that hunts down spelling mistakes, typos, and grammatical horrors, structure issues, alignments and what not. My special thanks to my beta reader (who is also synonym of a true friend) who never misses a chance to hunt me down on all those errors that shall not go in my book.

Besides this, my chirping bird who's chirps, songs, dances, Instagram reels, capoeira, mischiefs and pranks are always on the top of my head. She never misses a chance to extend her adolescent advice about my books and writings. Her innocence is the key to my smile and that makes me full charged up for my work. Loads of hugs and kisses to my child, (Chiya).

Grammarsaurus Rex* (metaphor of dinosaurs for grammar Nazis)

Furthermore, my sincere and honest thanks to all the readers who have made my other 2 books a hit and have criticized me to the fullest. This in turn is an insane feeling, but I love criticism and this does not stop me to write. I'm glad that I have honest readers around me who are a part of my journey.

My heart is with my well-wishers and the great personalities who have agreed to share foreword for my book.

Last but not the least, I'm extremely thankful to all my family members, friends, relatives, acquaintances who have motivated me to write more books. The best slice of this happiness is even if someone from them are not readers would support and inspire me to move ahead. My love to all of you.

Lastly, my gratitude will be unsaid if I don't thank my almighty and the universe for showing me light always.

Guilt – Right or Wrong?

Here I go solo,

Solo life,

Boy you can cool it down to chill

Just wanna be with you

But if you don't mind

Please let me be solo

"Craft the perfect life

The road to guilt

Isn't your destination"

The Real Truth About Guilt

Guilt is an emotion felt deep inside that has a twisted impact on our mind and heart. Well, that is difficult to infer, I know.

The power of guilt within us can't be underestimated, to get to know where we are heading to. Significantly understanding the actual power of this emotion would support your well-being to live a fair and joyous life.

Let us see a few questions which we all try to figure out in our daily lives and seek answers often.

What is the agenda of your life?

To live happily? To have an abundance of money?

To let your fear, go?

To have a beautiful and loving relationship?

To own a house?

To travel the world?

To become successful business owner?

Guilt – Right or Wrong?

The list is never-ending, and it varies from individual to individual. To compensate alongside the desires mentioned we tend to work on our actions and emotions simultaneously. While working on them and chasing our dreams human lives encounter situations when they feel stuck and tend to fall into the trap of guilt.

This section would try to convey how powerful guilt can be and what are its types. Also, how your mind generates this emotion within you knowingly or unknowingly.

#guilt has the power to build your life

If taken into right consideration

If not, it would hold you back from #growing

Thus, understanding it is a mandate.

Facts About Guilt

That wicked feeling of remorse takes a toll on your mental health. One shall know that guilt is the most common psychological feeling of humans, which is still under research.

It is that feeling which disturbs our sensitive wellbeing and signals us when our actions have produced damage to someone or otherwise. I would say the beauty of emotion called "guilt" is that it occurs in microbursts or brief signals. Conversely, it plays a vital role in our lives. We acknowledge guilt as a negative emotion that leads to dishonour, distress, mental stress, shame, emotional stress, regretful life, etc.

Guy Winch PhD mentioned something interesting about Guilt, check this out.

The Squeaky Whee - Before you can rightly find out why you are tormented with regret, you must originally learn about this emotion. Detailed knowledge of guilt can be logically astute and clear up many complications.

Guilt – Right or Wrong?

First and foremost, guilt's outset is completely mental. This routes to the track when people encounter this emotion when they admit they have provoked harm or are otherwise accountable for someone else's affliction. These observations can exist unheeding of whether or not the person is right or inaccurate. These troublesome thoughts later arouse the feeling that human beings refer to as guilt.

Theoretically, guilt is an emotional phenomenon that is a part of psychological studies. We tend to lose ourselves in guilt. This emotion is consolidated with shame and fear at times. This drives serious issues on mental health. There are extensive researches that show how this emotion of guilt swamps you, and leads to disaster.

Sharing the entire certainty of guilt may mitigate the feelings, so, for now, let's talk about guilt, as it is not a great feeling to nurture for human lives.

If we start by the definition, guilt is a feeling of justified blame for something. We tend to feel that we have earned it. In actuality, we have dealt with it as per the situations. Here, we feel that we have committed the correct act, as we do not want to do it, but we anyway perform the act. This emotion is complicated and

Guilt – Right or Wrong?

thinkers and psychologists are in a continuous quest to bring out the corrective actions and behaviours about guilt.

Like, for instance, I use to experience guilt when in childhood, for not attending to family functions and exaggerating about it to my mom. Making lame excuses for not going. I do not use to like them. I used to feel despairing and gloomy about the comments being made about my dress, body weight, too much bubbly and big buttocks, the list would on and on. But, I avoided gatherings for my joy and to also avoid embarrassing moments. But a lie is a lie.

You know at times to avoid something which gives you pain, "Guilt" may be factual. Although it took me a while understanding my worth and I stopped sprawling about it anymore in future, and this took span of years for me to realise this bitter truth. I felt good back then, guilt made me do something which probably is not correct and I did it for my justification. When we perform an action knowing it is not right, and yet offer a justification to it, becomes our guilt later in life.

So can it be right and wrong?

Guilt – Right or Wrong?

Guilt keeps our actions and moves in check, between the lines of right and wrong. It isn't such a terrible emotion if applied the right way with wisdom. Thus, keep a watch on your sentiments of guilt whenever popping in and question yourself whether it is destructive or if it's productive.

It takes joy from us. Initially, it may not seem like a big deal, but it does take all your positive energy drive. By conceding our feelings of guilt and working through them, we can improve our mental capacity and emotional wellbeing, and that my pal, is an advantage to everyone!

Remember while the guilt can be productive towards our goals but it can be the one that would keep you holding for a long time within you. This is unquestionably not good. The real truth about guilt is, it is both good and bad. But, that's all on us.

∞∞∞∞∞∞∞∞∞∞∞∞∞∞∞∞∞∞∞∞∞∞∞∞∞∞∞∞∞∞∞∞∞∞

Good Guilt

How would we determine guilt? We over and over again feel wrong and sinful about the things that are irrational in our lives.

"In a world that is growing and getting divided and atomized more and more, it may be guilt not empathy, that can bring people together. - Libby Copeland"

With this quote, if you see it is insinuated that with a high frequency of sympathy one can depreciate the level of sin. Good guilt is synonymous with sympathy and the close cousin empathy. Effort by Tina Malti, a psychology professor at the University of Toronto, advises that guilt may reimburse for an emotional deficit. Good guilt is related to the consciousness that makes us not perform any task which is not right for our mind. It is extremely disputable when it comes to guilt, weather it is right or wrong. Trillions of researches have been administered on proving how guilt behave in different human beings. It is not just restricted to humans; it is with animals as well. But with them it's a different way as they are speechless and so they use different actions to convey the same.

From the times of Sir Freud to Aristotle, studies have revealed that guilt works better in kids. Parents often teach kids how to guilt in a right way, as this prevents them not to indulge in thieves, robbery and any anti-social crime when they grow. *(proven studies have suggested – study by a psychologist, at Suffolk University professor Jane Bybee).*

Today numerous personages consider guilt as a dangerous emotion. Not to blame them, it is admittedly. But only in the self-help books. In actuals, it is psychologically proven that when treated with empathy – the close cousin, can lead to constructive actions in future.

For example – kids aged 2 years to 4 years old were requested for an experiment. They were put with a creative director in an open space, but the entrances and pathways were closed for the kids not to bypass. There was a huge building or a tower of blocks kept in the room which was for the creative director to shoot and to be used for filming purposes. While leaving the room the creative director said, please do not touch this building/tower, play aside. As the room was also loaded with plentiful toys on the other corners too.

Of course, they are kids, unquestionably it was bound to happen. So, the room got in a mess, a few kids blew away the tower, they tried to dismantle and make it again, and a few started playing with broken blocks. There were others who did not bother to touch the tower and played with the other toys kept in the room.

After an hour when the kids were called over on what happened in the room. Why and what all they did - kids responded, "I'm sorry". Others who claim to have smashed the building said "we had fun", and later started to rebuild it again. What do we observe here, is unlike other emotions children are not born with sadness, fear, anxiety, anger, guilt? All these sentiments emerge a bit later for them in life. When it comes to "I'm Sorry", it is like they are growing their own morals and for them, it is a pang of moral guilt. Kids are prone to guilt in a sorry format they consider as the moral norm. On the other side, the kids who broke the building and were trying to rebuild showed engaging behaviour that is a popsicle attitude. This shows their cooperative behaviour toward the act which is not at all a bad guilt or anything to worry for. As they are learning social and moral norms with constructive actions.

So, how do you teach good guilt? If a child spills milk, instead of scrutinising the child, say something like, "What a mess". What should we do about it? Don't tell them, what to do, let them figure it out. They'll presumably start cleaning it up. This helps kids to learn to feel blame and offence, but also to get past it away.

In general consciences, guilt still has a bad thump. It is considered to be one of the most uncomfortable emotions among the similar ones in behavioural sciences. For example, jealousy and anger and later depression is a subsequent consequence of bad guilt. Alright, let's understand bad guilt then.

Bad Guilt

Guilt, in other words, can help hold a symbiotic species together. It is a kind of social glue. Also, a person's guilt is relatable to the moral code. Regret is something you perceive typically when you do something wrong or you act upon anything which you shouldn't. This is an occurrence in your life where you exhibit misplaced, irrational, and misappropriate emotions. That becomes a pang of unhealthy guilt for you.

Like for example, you have been ripped in between the work-life balance, or you are dealing with some real toxic relationship, which you are eagerly wanting to end up with, but you can't. Here you may not be wrong in avoiding the relationship with a person or managing your work-life balance to the most beneficial equations so that you can give sufficient time to your family, friends and yourself.

But in executing so, you end up tasting remorse or misplaced. This is when you get comments from others which you do not like and for which you are perceived. They ask you to realise that you are not giving them enough which they deserve from you. Maybe the toxic relationship is not ending because of you – being said by your partner. Or when repeated claims are being thrown sarcastically on your actions, you feel bad, right? Yes, you do!

This engulfs you with the consciousness of weakness. Here, this guilt can be dangerous. As it entangles you and your mind. You might even try to avoid those moods thinking a bit positive and lighter on your part, but it does not leave you easy. Negative emotions seize you for a longer time, unlike positive ones. Here, if our emotions are unchecked it may lead to unhealthy guilt in us. This can have drastic consequences on our lives.

The bad guilt is like a bad guy. We have no control over the passions as our activities and mind is superlatively disturbed.

For instance, if you have just got a promotion in your job and your friend on the other side is going through a horrible setback in your career. You'd be happy about the success and promotion, however, you will be worried about your friend's bad times too. This friend happens to be your best friend, though, hence the disturbance gets severe and it converts into unhealthy guilt. You feel condemned about your own promotion

Guilt – Right or Wrong?

that happens to be at the wrong time as your lovely friend is undergoing a ruthless phase in his career. Here your guilt is irrational and unhealthy. You haven't done anything wrong, the actions are not in your control, and you have not created the circumstance. Hereafter you should not be feeling regretful, instead, stick with your bestie in these times.

∞∞∞∞∞∞∞∞∞∞∞∞∞∞∞∞∞∞∞∞∞∞∞∞∞∞∞∞∞

Survivor Guilt – The Epic

Let me share an extreme case with you of bad guilt: according to me the "survivor guilt" during the times of the COVID-19 pandemic has been one such example of bad guilt. People are losing their jobs and have lost all their work, while some who are working have "survivor guilt" and keep on feeling unashamed of the situation. They can't do much about it. Yet, guilty. One shall not feel guilty about everything which is going on around them. Especially when things are not in their hands. For this type of guilt, there is nothing much we can do except work on our minds and try changing the mind-set.

One tip to overcome this guilt: Use affirmation for a broad range of issues and situations like the above by saying: "I did my best with the knowledge and wisdom I had, because I know that humanity wins."

∞∞∞∞∞∞∞∞∞∞∞∞∞∞∞∞∞∞∞∞∞∞∞∞∞∞∞∞∞∞∞∞∞∞∞∞∞

The Art Of Guilt

Carrying out guilt is an art. Well, not really, but there is something positive about this emotion, which overpower our minds and actions. On a more widespread scale if a person's actions are not in the line with their reason, belief system or teachings then guilt stems into the roots. This holds them accountable for their actions and forces them to confess their wrong-doings.

What are the forces that make guilt such an obsessive phenomenon? Thinkers and psychologists have said that dealing with guilt is an art. Overlooking the factor, they also suggested that the affectionate relative of guilt is a shame. Particularly, Pia Mellody, John Bradshaw, Pat Carnes, and Claudia Black, have divided disgrace, by breaking it down into two main groups: healthy shame and toxic shame.

It is further described that healthy shame is the feeling of, "I have done something that goes against my rooted values and belief systems, and something for what I feel bad about," on the other hand toxic shame defines the feeling of, "I am characteristically blemished and imperfect and therefore undeserving of love and belonging."

This explicitly explains the art of guilt. Which is broadly into two divisions – healthy and unhealthy or good or bad.

Why it is also viewed as an art, is because it is a kind of mixed emotions and a composite grid of emotions that drift others in your bloodstreams. They come out with every action of yours and can take serious action like stealing, lying, robbing, murder and maybe worse. Here one thing is essential to notice that guilt also brews a variety of depressive and negative emotions, like sadness, grief, agony, stress, anxiety, loneliness, shame, etc.

Hence it is a convoluted framework and an exact explanation of this emotion in humans is still researched and surveyed. From clinical psychologists to researchers, to the psychopath, to the physiotherapist and other professionals – they have been trying to understand and infer the guilt emotions taking the base of Freudian view and theories.

Guilt – Right or Wrong?

The psychodynamic theory of Freud advises that we build defence mechanisms to protect us from the liability we would experience if we knew just how awful our wretched desires were. Precisely, Freud linked the feeling of guilt (as well as anxiety) to the Oedipal stage of psychosexual development. It is believed that young children, desire to have sex with their opposite-sex parents, is also a part of the guilt.

They attempt it in compulsive and obsessive behaviour, while later regret. Eventually, these attractions become swamped and converted into sexual attraction toward others of their age.

Conferring to Freud's disciple, Erik Erikson, this is a somewhat blurred view of Freud's stress on sexuality as the only dynamism in the expansion and therefore he took issue with Freud's notion of guilt.

Instead, there is a finding which believes that guilt first arises in life around ages 3-5 as the negative consequence of a period termed as "initiative vs. guilt." Children develop a strong sense of guilt at this age as the polar opposite of playfulness. They are also afraid to express themselves with their toys because they fear that if they showed their true emotions to their toys, they would leave them, or not play with them, and they would commit an unacceptable act. They grow up to be overly frustrated adults who constantly fear doing something for which they'd later feel guilty.

This is a psychological approach and findings of guilt and its study. Pointing this here is what I mean to say, it is not something that is a new emotion or can't be dealt with. Knowing the fact that it is not a straightforward feeling too, yet it can be understood and eliminated from our lives. This will eventually lead us to live a free and joyous life.

How to practice this craft, for us to be happy in our lives?

Honestly, there is no thumb rule to learn the art of guilt. As guilt is triggered by different perceptions and emotions one can't practice one said rule to overcome regrets in life. Different approaches work on different human's beings. However, the majority works for all though, as our mind can be conditioned and the human mind is powerful.

As human beings, we know the act of apologising. This works in our favour for most of the situations to remain guilt-free. Apologising seems to be the most difficult job to do for a herd of people. They feel rhapsodic to

Guilt – Right or Wrong?

bend down for their mistakes. Normally apologising or feeling sorry about what you have done and later apprehending that it has been developed into guilt is a common phenomenon. It is also seen that the sorrowful sentiment which comes out of this feeling is maximum times inappropriate and clumsy. People tend to get neurotic, would not look into the eyes, would fall short of words or even use unsuitable methods to convey their corporeal sorry. Seeking only sorry or saying forgive me, does not help if you are not feeling the pain and admitting that you have committed a mistake.

When in guilt it is essential to understand that where you went wrong (if you are in bad guilt), and what can you do to amend things around you or with the person inflicted with. Also do not take the burden of the legacy all alone, if you do so it becomes chaotic guilt.

You are not the one who goes through it, everyone does. Motivate yourself about the circumstances foreseen that are arising due to the regrets in you. Because time heals everything, and nothing remains the same forever except the universal energies, that are all within you.

Guilt – Right or Wrong?

I have given a short journal writing practice to understand the art of guilt and how you can deal with it. Do write your own experiences, while attempting. I'm sure you will feel better and consciously strong. Also, let me know in case you have any questions or something to discuss. (email is on the last page).

Guilt – Right or Wrong?

The Rational Approach To Guilt

If you don't like the psychodynamic approach to guilt, perhaps you'll find the cognitive explanation a bit more appetising. From a rational point of view, guilt is a sentiment that individuals experience because they're persuaded that they've triggered harm to others. In rational theory, thoughts cause emotions. The emotion of guilt follows directly from the thought that you are accountable for someone else's discomfort, whether or not this is the case.

People who continuously undergo guilt on a recurring basis, according to the cognitive perspective, wrongly suffer under the delusion that they have caused other people harm. Their negative emotion arises from their inclination to distort what happens to them and not to question the logic of their conclusions. The treatment often entails teaching people to rid themselves of their "automatic thoughts." This is a quite straight and clear treatment to move away from this emotion.

People who continually are bothered by guilt are also taught to recognize their "broken attitudes" so that they appreciate when they're going through such mental methods as catastrophizing (making the very most inadequate of a bad situation) or overgeneralizing (considering that if one bad thing happened, many more must have as well). This shall stop, this shall not pop up in the heads. The whole logical idea is about this.

In contrast to the psychodynamic view of guilt, the logical and more rational perspective gives the average person some evidence for fixing the drift to blame yourself for everything that goes wrong.

"If you change your thoughts, you can change your emotions."

The moment you apprehend that you're clumsily seeing yourself as making others suffer, you can rearrange your mental perspective and more realistically figure out your role in whatever grief came your way. This way it will help you to receive greater attention towards your deeds and you will be out from your difficult emotions swiftly.

Types Of Guilt

Guilt, a notoriously tricky concept to define, is an emotion and a condition that almost everyone encounters. Across all the definitions, guilt is linked to the devastation of a group's or a person's morals. The objective state of guilt leads to a situation in which a person has violated a rule of a religion, a state, a social group, or a community. In these scenarios, a person may be characterised and labelled "guilty."

The result normally may involve punishment or criticism. This kind of guilt may or may not include prejudiced or psychological guilt, which is the inner affective state in which a person feels highly worried, apologetic, and penitent.

Subjective guilt may result from infringing the internalized moral standards. Both types of guilt are paralleled to morality in social contexts or relationships. It is closely associated with natural guilt. In the largest of situations, a person classified as objectively "guilty" is likely to suffer from the internal embarrassment of being a transgressor, as well as from the anticipation of punishment. When people are defendant of being guilty, they may undergo from subjective guilt, even when the tag has been demarcated unfairly.

Clear distinction of this notorious emotion is not yet a mandate but there is specific guilt which we all go through in our lives: let's dive in!

Neurotic Guilt

Unreasonable guilt, is when guilt turns sour. It can lead to fervent obsessions, depressive tendencies, and physical symptoms if it's not addressed. While most guilt is organic, it is often conditioned by external factors — which means with the right attitudes, it can be unlearned. To unlearn this unreasonable guilt, you must know the signs. Guilt is tangled with other dysfunctions, and separating them can be a challenge. Understanding guilt's role in disorders like obsessive-compulsive disorder (OCD) and depression, along with its physical symptoms, can help you mark its signs and learn how to overcome extreme guilt. The bitter feelings from which psychoneurotic suffer are most commonly comprised of hatred, humiliation, incompetence, inferiority, envy, greed -- as well as guilt.

Let's see what a Canadian primal therapist, Janice Berger, explains in her excellent book, Emotional Fitness "that not all guilt is neurotic but that a lot of it is."

Guilt – Right or Wrong?

Moral guilt means that something candidly wrong has been done and a feeling of guilt is therefore sustained. The baffling percentage of guilt that bothers us, is neurotic guilt and it is not easy for the sufferer of neurotic guilt to separate the two types of guilt from each other as they both feel the same. Both types of guilt are often conferred as a combination of both rational and irrational guilt.

It is also seen that numerous conflicts provoke guilt and sin where religion is involved. Religion plays a role in instilling sin into its followers. Apparently no religion teaches us to destroy or humiliate others. It would be quite impracticable ever to determine the exact amount of psychic damage which has been done by the cliché risen from every priesthood. Because God for sure does not wish to serve his children with neurosis and psychosis.

Neurotic guilt starts from home and instigates at early age. Supporting guilty children doesn't mean those parents do it in a deliberately in a boisterous way. It's not about letting the kid know that it's his fault that the milk was spilt; it is much more sedate than that. The drilling of our mind toxins is usually a do-it-yourself job. Trying to make sense of our world from the sources of awareness, we simply settle quite early - like in the crib (a child thinks) - why we don't deserve the amount of love and concern that we need. No words need to be expressed here. The infant simply decides that "it's gotta be my fault" and henceforth the seed of neurotic guilt is planted.

In the nutshell, when it is about one's self, more spilt milk and more "going to confession" just strengthen the feeling. Later, as we age and our justifications weaken and any incidence which has the slightest feeling coincide to our early deprivation of love and needs, taps into our very early neurotic outcomes which we had about ourselves as the guilt tape converts in replay mode.

"Being sympathetic to the effects of every action, bewildered by possibly making the "wrong" decision, Low self-esteem, putting others before yourself until it's damaging, avoiding your full range of emotions, is Neurotic guilt."

Toxic or Free-Floating Guilt

Toxic guilt is what happens when natural guilt decays. It exhibits a nagging feeling of prevalent but nonspecific sadness as if your whole life has something wrong with it. This type of free-floating guilt is the most troublesome of the kinds. It is the hardest to deal with because it arises from crawling patterns, or sanskaras (the societal morals that are induced in us, not knowing right or wrong), stuck in your subconscious. How can you appease your sin or forgive yourself for something when you don't know what it is which you did? Or when you believe that what you did is basically irreversible?

To some degree, this unusual type of guilt seems to be an unintended by-product of Judeo-Christian culture, a residue of the doctrine of original sin. (index). Yogic texts like the Bhagavad Gita and the Yoga Sutra do not identify nonspecific guilt. On the other hand, they do say quite a bit about sin, karma, and how to dodge or purify infractions. Although even the toxic guilt is not explicitly mentioned in most traditional lists of yogic obstacles, the yogic teachings do offer help on it.

Guilt – Right or Wrong?

Normally we experience toxic guilt in two ways. First, it can simply be there, like a character in your personality, a foul feeling that can instinctively come into consciousness at certain times, causing you to feel bad or unworthy. Second, it can be triggered by outside factors, whether by a mistake you make or somebody's mistrust. If you're carrying a toxic guilt backpack, it doesn't take much to stimulate it. A slip-up at the office, a fight with your beloved, quarrel with your boss, or a call from your mother, your kid's reaction to your income - can do the job to alleviate the burden of your backpack.

So, it's essential to learn how to recognize feelings of toxic guilt so that they no longer feed you from the inside. Toxic guilt often has pedigrees in primary childhood days: Slipups that your parents or educators, pickled as a big deal, for instance - spiritual training, especially the kind of training that instils original sin, can fill us with guilty feelings that have no real foundation. Some believes in the concept of reincarnation, like the idea that our existing circumstances are defined by patterns set in past lives. These notions see the toxic guilt as the karmic residue of past-life actions stored in our ingenious system.

Guilt – Right or Wrong?

One ancient text of Tibetan yoga, called The Wheel of Sharp Weapons, (index) lists past sins that are specific to the present-day difficulties. They denote that these have been evolved from the past and provides remedies for alleviating them. Multiple purist yogic practices, particularly daily chanting and mantra repetition, selfless service (karma yoga), and offerings are recognised medicine for these guilty feelings. But there's no question that toxic guilt can also come from an acquired accumulation of specific, unrepaired harm that you've created in this life. When you've racked up a few unpleasant moments of self-betrayal, or even when you ignore to call your parents or get enough consistent exercise, you can accumulate a fair amount of free-flowing guilt.

Moreover, a yogi on a path of awakening will often generate an exquisitely ethical conscience. Once you begin to hold yourself to the ethical standards of the spiritual path, it becomes more active to let yourself get away with indifferent or malicious behaviour. At the same time, you may still have some old habits of procrastination and unconsciousness. So, despite your best purposes, you sometimes do things that you know aren't good for yourself or other people, and feel guilty. But if you are prepared to look more intensely, you'll apparently find that your sense of toxic guilt has very little to do with anything that you did. That, paradoxically, is what makes it so lethal.

Let it go the toxic guilt - We need to work with toxic guilt not only to lighten the pain it creates but also because expanded feelings of guilt build up and associate themselves to any current crime, even very minor ones, causing negative self-talk and sick feelings that are out of proportion to the misdemeanour.

Drowning Under Bestie's Guilt

Friends are precious. Every relationship starts with friendship. Being friends is the base of a rock-solid relationship, be it – spouses, love birds, relatives, family, siblings, every relation gets nurtured with friendship. While at one end this is the cutest thing to adorn in our lives, yet it is one of the murkiest to handle. There is a thin line which if crossed due to lack of accurate communication can tear the lovers apart.

How often you feel guilty about your besties. How often do you say sorry and apologise for what you might have done with them? How often your actions decide your move rather than communication and understanding.

A bond that is not to be broken shall be tied with trust and communication. More importantly, ego shall not come in between. I lost a friend because of this misunderstanding, hence know the burden. A true friend is a treasure and I know how I feel to lose a person because of these shady things. Heartbreaks are nothing about losing a comrade for life. Here, something about friendship guilt.

Guilt – Right or Wrong?

Our bond was pure and we both shared like-mindedness. John and I were working together on an internship project. His friend Andrew, quite a cool guy, was his best friend since childhood. They both shared a crazy relationship. We wanted one more guy in our team for the project. The deadline was on the head and we weren't able to sort it out for anyone else as the other teams were frozen.

We pooled in Andrew, knowing the fact that he is quite a weirdo too. He is bestie to John but was not that great with girls. Meaning he had a habit of being flirting with girls often. Getting into an affair for a shorter period and breaking up. Hooks up were common for him. He was one of those who was not into great connection with girls. I have heard a lot of stuff about him in college. I was initially advised by my fellow mates, not to be his friend and keep a distance from Andrew. Of course, we have to complete the internship project before the deadline and I did not listen to any one of those. We moved ahead and I thought I will have to be with John more as I was more comfortable with him and we use to share regular substance and stuffs. For me, he was the bestie and the most considerate human I know.

Guilt – Right or Wrong?

Since childhood, I have been with girls always and never got a chance to gel up with guys. Hence when I went to college, I was sceptical of being comfortable with boys. Initially, I was driven by fear later John and his group approached me to be friends. I felt at eased and we continued to be together for long hours and chilling out in the cafeteria, etc. Gradually john and I drew closer and we shared our lives in detail.

John was brought up by a single mother as his dad left when he was just a kid. He was significantly close to her mother and shared an unconditional bond. He aimed to make his mom happy and become super successful for her to be proud of him. Maybe this bond made him respectful towards women. He was like a coconut, hard from outside and soft from inside.

We all three usually used to work at my place. My room was big enough and there was no other disturbance surrounding us. Post-college we all three used to work for hours on the project. John was an intelligent student and his clarity of concepts helped us a lot in our project. Andrew used to work more on experiments and trial and error theories. Surprisingly I like doing experiments more rather than documentation, which was in actual my part in the project. As the deadline approached nearer we all three geared up for the project completion. At times we got on to the sleepovers at my place, due to long working hours. This project was very important for all of us, as based on this our off-campus placements would matter.

Andrew and I got a bit closer (which I never thought) and enjoyed doing experiments. We kind of chilled more than John often. John witnessing this do not have any issue as my bond with him as a true friend for life was sturdy. Anyway, this went on and just a day before our project submission, we all three were set to make the final report, review the research outcomes, check the documentation and proceed to submit.

John left a bit early as his mom wasn't well for a couple of days and he has to be with her and took her to see a doctor. He was not worried about the project now, knowing that we have got this on the completion. Andrew and I assured him not to worry about anything just leave and stay with his mom.

Andrew and I completed the rest of the job with minor revisions here & there and finished the entire presentation and report for the final submission. I rested for a while asking him to please take dinner himself. Being dead tired after day-long work I took a nap. Andrew post-dinner rested for while near me. Good night… the night ended.

The next morning was not so good. Anxiety hovered over me inside, out. I was in deep pain and my heart broke, because Andrew mistreated me. He tried to get on over me last night when I was sleeping. He kissed me forcibly, touched my body parts by his wrongdoings. Repeatedly yelling no, it's wrong, what are you doing, stop, and on and on. Nothing stopped, I was touched on my breasts and kissed again n again. I tried to pull him off, but he didn't and said – it is ok, chill, it is just for fun babe. We are friends, this much is allowed. You also enjoy and partake, it will be fun, and no strings attached. I was devastated by his thoughts and never knew that he would attempt something like this.

When I yelled and shouted for my mom and told him that I would complain to John and the college. As I announced that I'm calling my mom upstairs, he just threw me the way and pushed me on the bed and said you will pay for it. You are threatening me on everything, I was just asking for a fun time/one-night-stand. What is wrong with this, he shouted. With his anguished mind, he left my place.

Guilt – Right or Wrong?

"But until then the damage was done."

It was the day of the project submission. I woke up with deep pain and remorse. I was feeling emotionally broken and I texted John immediately to tell him about everything. However, I stopped thinking about the project submission. I somehow waited for our submission. We all met in college and submitted our project. I controlled my emotions at that very time in front of John and Andrew. I felt terrible and broken, my face was placed in pain, John asked what's wrong. I ignored it, thinking for the right time to speak as I was not sure how John will react as – John and Andrew were good friends too. It was tough for me. Post submission I took John to the other side and shared everything exactly the way it happened. Thinking in my mind that John shall Support, as I was telling the truth.

He was stunned and I knew he would be; it was hard for him to know that Andrew did something like this. With a pause to process what I have said, John said I don't think he must have done it this way to you. However, I will speak with him and get things clear. But if he has done this horrendous job then God only save him from my wrath. It was disturbing and traumatizing for me. Eventually, I was the barrier of guilt in me forever because John figured out that Andrew did wrong with me. Without my permission, he touched me and tried to get sexual.

With no consent from me, John understood that Andrew was at fault which he should not have done and would have respected her dignity. The trust broke, the relationship becomes bitter, we all three went to our caves for quite a long period. It was hard for John to let him go like this. They could not be friends with the dent in their hearts. And I left alone with guilt in me for breaking the friendship of all of us. But I knew that truth was important to come out, if I would have hidden it in me, that would be wrong and I would be living with inflammation of pain in me.

Many seasons passed... John and I came to terms and are friends again, but no sign and news of Andrew.

Let It Go!

Friendships are beautiful and there is a thin line between trust and blind friendship. A friend shall be the mirror of a friend. At times the trust becomes blind, for not to see the truth and the friendship becomes sour.

Guilt – Right or Wrong?

The best thing about a true friend is that they recognize you without having to say a lot. And this holds both ways. With your bestie, your understanding is such that you can pick up from where you left. Negative reactions and actions can lead to inflammatory relationships. Certain unbalances in communications and thinking if it develops over time, increases the chances of cheating and ruining the relationship.

We somehow expect friendships to be forever. The break-ups in friendships, challenge our vision of who we are, but do not let the guilt to pour in. Because you are not the person who is responsible for other's actions. Leave this scary thought and forgive the sins. Because always remember that if in a situation where you have to save yourself or save your friendship, I would say choose yourself. Friendship is always between two peers, but if you would not attain that balance then it will shatter.

Natural Guilt

Assume you feel guilty about immediate action and explicit deeds, like putting a dent in the car that you have borrowed from your friend or you lying to your boyfriend about where you were last night. That's what I call natural guilt. Here, you can say that you're suffering from natural guilt because it's locally produced: It connects to your actions in real, like in present times. Natural guilt can be uncomfortable, especially if there's serious injury involved. But even if what you did was bad, local guilt is curable. You can make amends. You can ask for forgiveness, pay your debt, and determine to change your behaviour. And once you fix things, the guilt should evaporate (if not, see the section "Toxic Guilt").

Natural guilt obeys a functional purpose, and it seems to be hard-wired into the nervous system. It's an organic alarm bell that helps you recognise unethical behaviour and correct the direction. Natural guilt prompts you to call your mother with whom you haven't spoken for a month or leave your phone

Guilt – Right or Wrong?

number on the car when you ran the bumper of a parked car.

Natural guilt, some social scientists believe, arrives from our capacity to empathize with others' suffering, and it's one of the reasons we have things like social safety nets and movements for social justice. When you have a healthy relationship with your guilt, you don't struggle over guilty feelings. Instead, you use them as signals to change your behaviour.

You handle your regret over spending too much by holding back. If your guilt comes from accepting your part in some common wrongdoing, racial injustice or some other form of abuse of one group by another, you look for a way to help in bringing the change. And if your guilt comes from something you can't do much about, like the working mother's guilt, single parent guilt, the bread runner of the family, about not being the one to pick up her kid from school every day, then do practice giving yourself a break.

Much Needed! Isn't It?

It is said that natural guilt has a shadow side. It often turns into a major tool of parental and social control. An old joke captures this perfectly. How many Jewish

Guilt – Right or Wrong?

mothers does it take to screw in a light bulb? None: "Don't worry, I'll just sit here in the dark." But it's not just mothers (Jewish or otherwise) who manipulate us through guilt. Spouses and partners do, too. So do religions, spiritual groups, and tribes and even yoga tribes.

Have you ever been guilt-tripped by a vegan friend who caught you eating salmon? Natural guilt is going in an off-beam direction when it's too heartlessly fixed or used as a defence of control, then it can quickly become toxic. When that happens, we find ourselves in the state of constant low-grade suffering that I call Toxic Guilt, which is a penetrating feeling of being "wrong" or flawed in some basic way.

∞∞∞∞∞∞∞∞∞∞∞∞∞∞∞∞∞∞∞∞∞∞∞∞∞∞∞∞∞∞∞∞∞

Feeling Regretful Can Be A Barrier In Self-Growth

"No one is perfect in this world. It is the most common proverb we all are aware of since our childhood. Even our great grandparents have been telling us this to make us feel more confident and secure in this mad world."

Agree? Or Disagree?

Well, this story is a beautiful narration of a couple (as parents) who have just started understanding the world of kids.

Yeah, I happen to know one such couple who have recently started their journey as parents. Of course, having the child was their choice. When I say their choice, it is both the mom and the father. Imperative to note that both share expanse of emotions and carry immense thoughts (irrespective of gender) while taking or going for this decision. If you have got this, you are lucky as I'm known to many who did not get privilege of being a parent to select as a choice. So, if you got this bliss, you shall nurture it with love.

Guilt – Right or Wrong?

So, they have a kid now, a beautiful girl named Muskan. As she deserves this name for her divine smile. Parenthood is not an easy responsibility to carry on. The difficult decisions that parent need to take while working, and then parenting simultaneously take a real hell on the heads. As said being a parent is a tough job, and it is a 24/7-hour job.

I feel that parents' guilt is like a cultural epidemic, yet highly transmissible.

Well, they thought it would be hard, but certainly not would have thought to be a mess. They were expecting it to be enjoyable, yes daunting at times, but certainly not an emotional turmoil. They both thought that they would cope with all coming their way.

…The mom took maternity from the job, hoping that the father would take it post 6 months when wife's leaves get over. This is how they both thought to manage time and work for the kid. Sadly, later the father could not manage to take leaves and was he incompetent, due to the company's HR policies. Although many organizations still don't have the option of maternity and paternity leave, which is a pain to bring up the baby in nuclear families.

Guilt – Right or Wrong?

Thus, the father was upset for not helping the mother and paying much attention to the kid as needed. For he is the bread earner, the responsibility was double, as she could not resume work back soon. Now all these cumulative thoughts, of not being able to take the paternity leave for his wife and kid and the overheads made him feel terrible and took him into his guilt.

Not just this, the mother on the other side, kept getting the feeling of rejection with due course of time. She is an independent woman who was thrashed due to not resuming the office. She even tried to put the baby in day-care. The fussy baby could not manage. As babies have their reflux to actions for settling in the given situation. Thus, she has to wait for a few months more for the kiddo to properly settle in the day-care.

It grew harder for both of them to manage, finances, homecare, work front, attention to the baby and each other. Seemed like their life is not going to a happy place. Both of them started feeling that they were not ready for parenthood and are not able to do justice to the baby as well. This remorse got stuck in them and their relationship seems to go for a toss. Parent's guilt took over.

Guilt – Right or Wrong?

Adjusting to parenthood and a new lifestyle is not easy for the parents. And believe me, it is not only for first-time parents. This emotion is similar for the parents of the second or the third child. The mixed bag of emotions and frustration makes life emotionally muddled and confused.

Understand that life matters too, your relationship is also important. It has to be flourished mentally for you to give best to your children. Probably it is good that child witnesses all your actions while growing. When you love someone, your entire world revolves around that person, here Muskan was everything for them. But new challenges of parenthood confused their pre-conditioned notions. Eventually, their journey becomes bitter because of their regrets.

"Parental guilt can be internalized or misinterpreted in a way that it seems to be unhealthy. The sooner it comes; the faster it has to let go."

Let It Go!

Let go of the feeling of regret as soon as it develops. Expressing guilt is not wrong or getting the feeling of remorse is not wrong, but letting it go is crucial. You can't let your guilt take over your current emotions to a distress level. Earlier in this book, we have seen that guilt can aggravate different emotions like anger, and this can be cruel in any relationship. It is very easy to get stuck in feelings of guilt. However, moving out of it immediately is the best thing. Do not forget that to take care of people who are dependent on you, you first have to be joyous. So, kill it, the moment it appears.

"When fear questions you to emphasis on what's missing, focus your attention to what's plentiful in life."

Existential Guilt

Our guilty feeling could also be social or political or moral. This is the guilt you feel when you see pictures of animals in a pen, which then reminds you about their sufferings which they might undergo in reality etc., or when you read about the suffering in Yemen, or when you see international border war zones, or the sufferings of refugees or identify the progressive opportunity of your life compared with the lives of many others. This is termed existential guilt. Existential guilt is quite tangible, and even practical.

Why? Because there is essentially no way to live life on earth without having some sort of negative impact on the lives. Whether it's the birds who lost their homes when trees were cut down for your premises to build or a brand new skyscraper; or the plants you crush while walking in nature; or the fact that your child got a space in a great public/private school, and lots of your friends' children didn't, or you have earned a brand-new Mercedes while others at your squad didn't own.

Guilt – Right or Wrong?

Existentially, often, the resources or the utilities which we use to live, or even to live simply, are not blessed to others or they are not even available to them as basics. This is a sheer example of existential guilt.

Years ago, an attractive, rich woman told one of her mentors that she is grieving from intense guilt and despair. Her mentor replied by asking, what have you done for life? Have you ever put a bagel on a tree and walked away? Her guide's question lingered with her for years. Not only because it was pointing out an awful gesture or it is arresting, but also because of the essential wisdom behind it. That woman's guilt complex was in part existential, and existential guilt can be relieved only by making unconditional offerings to life.

It's easy to understand why a person might feel a burden of existential guilt. The Vedic thinkers, whose astuteness is at the core of all the yogic traditions, taught that we all have definite rudimentary debts to our ancestors, to the earth, to our educators, to Universe, to God, and to everyone who's facilitated us. When we don't pay those debts, we undergo existential guilt.

Guilt – Right or Wrong?

On the other hand, our modern liberal society, with its strong individualism, broken families, and consumerist attitude toward spirituality, beckons existential guilt. It is because many of us, or I must say, most of us, are not taught how to respect life, how to respect time, how to obey the existential rules of life, or simply the basic gestures that honour the web of life. It can involve numerous things, like not only the conscious environmental practice or sustainable living, but also about heart touching practices like inviting guests to your table; sharing food with poor people, help animals, being compassionate towards the needy, giving service to the community and donating a part of your income; taking care of elders, and so on and so forth.

Once we can recognize a painful feeling like guilt and identify its type, it becomes easier to work with it. Certain type of guiltiness need amends because the awkward feeling points out our failure to live up to our values. Hence the best is to let go.

Effects Of Guilt

The psychosomatic consequences of remorse can be advantageous when they encourage a person to make adjustments in their behaviour towards themselves and others. But at other times they can cause anguish. Studies has indicated that guilt and depression are often linked. Research also suggests that anxiety, as well as obsessive-compulsive disorder (OCD), can be related to feelings of guilt or shame.

When a person can't resolve a mistake, guilt can carry on until they have the chance to make amends. Guilt emerging from an activity that can't be repaired, such as when a person believes they indirectly caused another's death, can have a lasting, negative impact on life. Psychoanalysis healing can often help a human address these emotions and reframe their state of mind about what happened. This is when therapist work on mind conditioning, but if you can do it on your own with strong mental and meditative procedures, nothing like it.

Guilt – Right or Wrong?

Another effect of guilt is a guilt complex. This is tenacious guilt that occurs over a harm, which a person believes might have caused to others due to them. Intentionally you may not have done anything brutal to others, but they live in fear that they might end up doing the similar thing again, or believe that they are always making mistakes and can't do anything right. It is like a phobia of hurting people. Guilt complex can be linked with anxiety and shame. It is also related to a person's childhood memories and actions: When parents are exceedingly disapproving or suppress their praise towards their kids, children may recurrently feel guilty for what they see as their "badness or wrong attitude towards life." The best is to talk to them and try to appreciate small things, which will make them feel worthy of their actions.

∞∞∞∞∞∞∞∞∞∞∞∞∞∞∞∞∞∞∞∞∞∞∞∞∞∞∞∞∞∞∞∞∞

Dealing With Guilt

There's no magical cure for excessive guilt. Defeating it takes a lot of harmonious emotional work, just as with any strong emotion. Regular appreciation and reflection are two touchstones for overcoming guilt. Ask questions to yourself like, "What is making me feel guilty?" and "What actions or thoughts are happening because of my guilt?"

Additionally, positive thinking and fortification can help overcome guilt. Changing the verbosity for your thoughts can reconstruct your outlook on the source of your guilt. For example; change "I should" or "I could" to something more positive, like "I get to," "I deserve," or "I can" when appropriate. This will boost your confidence and your mind get regular positive affirmations.

And this is where yoga knowledge offers one of its most worthy and life-changing gifts. The yoga institution has numerous specific remedies for spirits of guilt *(See The Yogi's Guide to Self-Forgiveness for specifics)*. But the most magnificent guilt-busting attitude of the yogic tradition provides us with the fundamental recognition of our essential morality.

Tantric traditions particularly are known for looking at the world through a lens that sees all life as fundamentally spiritual. Your attitude towards your guilt will undergo a huge shift when you begin to follow spiritual teachings. Instead of thinking human beings are intrinsically flawed, it will teach you to look beyond your flaws and helps you to know your deeper perfection.

Here's a tale from, Swami Muktananda, which used to tell a story that I think illuminates the difference between these two ways of viewing ourselves. There were once two monasteries, each situated near to a big city. In one monastery, the students were taught that human beings are sinners and that powerful alertness and penance are the only ways the students could dodge their wicked tendencies. In the other monastery, the pupils were fortified to have faith in their essential goodness and to trust their hearts.

One day, a young man from each of these monasteries decided that they needed a respite from monastic life for a while. Each boy snitched out his dorm window and hitched a ride to the nearby city. They found a chic party happening, and ended up spending a sensual night with a woman in a brothel. Next morning, the young man from the "sinner" monastery was able to overcome with gruelling repentance. He thought, I've trip over irreversibly from my path of salvation. There's no point of me going back. He didn't return to his monastery as he was not able to face the remorse and soon became part of a street gang.

The second boy also woke up with a relic. But his response to the situation was very diverse. He thought; That was not as satiating as I imagined it would be, and said to himself. "I don't think I'll do that again anytime soon in my life." Then he went back to his monastery, climbed in the window, and was rebuked for niggling out at night.

What is the learning, my teacher would say that when we believe, that we are sinners and have done something hideous, a very small slip of our action can send us spiralling into a configuration of self-destructive actions? But when we realise and understand, as the yoga sages articulate, that we are profoundly divine, that we are all Buddha's, it's much easier to forgive ourselves for the bad or unskilful things we do. It's also easier to change our behaviour.

Guilt – Right or Wrong?

Hence the real solution to our sticky guilty feelings is to distinguish, over and over again, that the light of God's love is the main source which illuminates our heart.

∞∞∞∞∞∞∞∞∞∞∞∞∞∞∞∞∞∞∞∞∞∞∞∞∞∞∞∞∞∞∞∞

Wipe It Out - Wipe The Slate Clean

The most significant part about guilt is to wipe it out like a clean slate. Consideration is one of the steps on the path to meditation. It allows the mind to pacify into the state of silence essential for meditation – it allows your thoughts to come up into awareness for your mind, body and emotional system to heal, for you to make a judgment of your experiences and put them into someplace on your soul's pathway. Then you can wipe the slate clean and face the future.

Guilt – Right or Wrong?

"In its healthiest form, guilt is a moral compass that guides us."

Estranged Within – Estranged Guilt

How much do we know about parenting? How much do we understand childhood? The feeling of shame and guilt can come from estrangement too. No matter how hard you try to be a good parent or you dig onto the parenting books under the deep sun, just to make sure that you bring up your child at your best. But what if the shame or guilt is coming from your children.

This story is about a child who faced estrangement from the family and gradually ends up being trapped in the feeling of remorse. Guilt is that feeling when we feel that we have done something wrong, but who decides that what is right and what is wrong and how do we come to a conclusion.

Jack, the guy who's born in a big family of around 8 members including his parents. He being this hyperactive, super-smart child since a kid. So, is it wrong? Nah...

Gradually with time he went into sports and played for teen football clubs in Florida. He was quite joyful. He wasn't inclined to studies much, which seem to be an obvious thing for him because he admirably plays soccer. But this thing does not go well with other family members. The cousins used to bully him for his sport and his parents under the pressure would insist him to study well so that he could go into an ivy league university.

Unfortunately, he did not have a great reputation in the family. But who will goanna decide this reputation, isn't it? He had an alcoholic uncle in the house and creepy cousins. The usual scene is quarrels, fights, no one getting on the terms with each other, abusive relationships and similar. Like these. Under these circumstances jack always thought about killing someone, he got this feeling while he was growing and once an adult this emotion prominently hovered his mind.

Amidst all this, his parents were casual and supportive in his deeds. They choose their son overall. But you know the pressure, the resistance of other family members tends to lead Jack towards estrangement. This happens year by year, not in a moment. He realised that his fundamentalist Christian parents were different from those of his uncles and aunts, yet they share the obsession to the same degree. Like for example jack's mother once told him that I'm hurting you because I have to, it is for your good, and I would do it again in future if needed, as this will be only for your good. As a child, it got stuck in there as hidden memory.

In a family where you lose your freedom of speech and have to struggle for every single emotion to express, it becomes tough to survive. And that's when you realise the need to run away and find your own space. This also happens when you find your solace and learn to deal with chronic feelings around you. When you are in a situation of fear and scared of being an extrovert, this takes a toll on your mental and physical activities. Jack dealt with all this and gradually could not get over the claustrophobic situation in his house.

When his schooling, graduation and his soccer everything got affected, he realised this has to change as he was feeling suffocated. Jack got sandwiched between his life's aspirations and his family's. When his efforts to stick around with his sisters and brothers, uncles and aunts and of course his parents failed, for many times now, he decided to leave. He used to ask himself what is that which I did wrong or have said something wrong to my mother or my family members. His go-to places were certainly guilt and depression.

Guilt – Right or Wrong?

Hence, he decided to take the devastating decision of being estranged from the family for good. Who will decide this was the right move or not? It is a very common question to ask yourself or even if you ask your friend about it, how will they evaluate and confirm you, on what is right and wrong or whether getting estrange from your family is right.

Years passed and jack was neutral towards his life. He had no anxiety and depression. He was living the life of his own choice. He still asks his wife, whether I'm a bad person, whether I have done something wrong to hurt my family or my parents. I loved them but I can't hurt them and can't go back to the abusive and traumatising relationships in my life. Despite all the awareness I keep judging myself for being estranged from my family. I think I'm at a bruised place as I see the judgement coming from the societal lens. I feel I'm a misguided person who is at shame and guilt.

I could go on… but it has to stop.

Let It Go!

Guilt is often the sentiment that escorts other grief-related feelings. This is one of the whys and wherefores, it is so grim to comprehend. It is also easy to confuse the experience of guilt with the experience of regret. Both are reactions that can befall when we are trying to make sense of the loss encountered. If you are part of the type of family where you feel the only available option to you is to estrange yourself, it's unfortunate and nobody would choose to be in that situation.

In actual, it is your decision to make and going down that route does not make you a bad or mistaken person. Once you have come to terms with estrangement, most people realise that they have found a sense of peace and relief that was unattainable whilst they were part of their toxic family and can begin the process of healing.

Do not forget that we are humans and we have this deep desire to be surrounded by our family or extended families. It is always there and will remain because of our civilizational structure. But when you challenge yourself to remain away from toxic situations in your

Guilt – Right or Wrong?

life, you shall not feel guilty about it. It is your world, your choice and you have to take the responsibility to sustain it. You are not a possession to anyone and your test is to have courage and clear thinking. This will cease the feeling of guilt.

In a survey of 1,600 separated parents and grandparents, it is found, that parents explained their child's estrangement for reasons often quite different from those commonly cited by estranged adult children. For example, while much has been written about the way that intoxicating or mentally ill parents affect children, a similarly recognized adult child might become alienated because of an incapability to manage the ordinary slings and arrows of family life.

When asked one young adult about her lingering feelings of fretfulness, she didn't mention the long hours she worked for Uber to make ends meet while she took lessons at the local college, her struggle finding reasonable childcare for her toddler as a single mother, or her worry about her capability to finish college and have a livelihood. Instead, she impugned her parents for her feelings of anxiety and lack of confidence. This is something which we humans transpire to do when put in given situations.

From this point, cutting off interaction with a parent is an attempt of refinement. It's a way of saying that the restrictions in the individual were either put there by the parent or 'triggered' by paternal communication. It permits one to hold on to a self-assessment as idyllic and without limitations, accrediting one's problems to childhood experiences or chemical imbalances rather than larger communal influences.

For example, take Teresa, a 25-year-old woman who plays the flute for the San Francisco Concerto (details changed to protect confidentiality). Throughout her childhood, her mother was extremely involved in her training – taking her to school and competitions, cheering her to practise when she was young until she became old enough to do so without her help. The mother designates herself as following her daughter's desire to get into a viable conservatory and play with an orchestra, both of which the daughter fortunately accomplished.

Last year, Teresa suddenly went 'no contact' after her therapist suggested that her mother likely suffered from a narcissistic personality disorder. To her mother, Teresa mentioned: You cared little less about my contentment than my just being a little mock-up of you.

Guilt – Right or Wrong?

I've realised that I'm a purist and feel like nothing is ever sufficient. If you had let me alone, I would be a lot happier. Being around you just retells me of all of those years I have spent.

The work with the family didn't confirm the verdict of the mother as a narcissist. Yet, the high level of parental participation that parents characteristically undertook over the past four decades can produce its problems. In the practice of healing, Teresa, found that some adult children estrange themselves because they know no other way to feel separate from their anxious and involved parents than to reject them.

Adult children might also want to practice detachment because parent anticipates more familiarity or accomplishment than the adult child can endure. According to the survey 'Culture of American Families (2012) conducted by the Institute for Advanced Studies in Culture, almost three-quarters of today's parents of school-age children say they eventually want to be their children's best friends; only 17 per cent disagree.

"Blame is not a magnitude of this sentiment."

∞∞∞∞∞∞∞∞∞∞∞∞∞∞∞∞∞∞∞∞∞∞∞∞∞∞∞∞∞∞∞∞∞∞∞

Bitter Sweet Sour

I wish I would have stopped her from not going. I wish I would have kissed her one last time. I wish I would have understood her one last time. I wish I would have heard her heart out. I wish, the darkness shall eliminate the pain that immersed the two of us. This, when destroyed four of us.

Well, it is not a love triangle or some sort of horrible love scene that you might have thought of. It is life in real. How many times it happens that we indulge ourselves in a **compulsive relationship**. Not even understanding the consequences. But, do we know that we are not the only ones to get trapped into compulsive relationships, which initially seemed perfect. One aspect of a compulsive relationship or affection is right-doing too. It can be fruitful in future. Because, we tend to feel stuck at first, but later that becomes our world.

For example, relationship with your pet. You may not be an animal person and is not willing to share your share of attention and love with a new member of your family i.e. a pet. Here, one can't compel or can't just

Guilt – Right or Wrong?

leave from the situation as one who has adopted an animal is fond of them. In these scenarios, you are bound to accommodate the existence. This gradually becomes your habit and you will not realise until this compulsive relationship became your life.

What I mean to infer is all gripping behaviours are not destructive and does not lead you to any kind of regret in your life. Of course, the number of these associations are significantly less. Here there is no need of letting a feeling go. As with time the bond nurtures and remain with us forever.

I met a man during my travel to India, he was from Israel. He was a musician by profession and when I saw him playing the guitar, I jammed and tuned with him. After a while, we started sharing some travel talks and that was when I realised that how deep pain, he is in. There is something that is bothering him to the core. We shared Himalayan Maggie together and I thought to ask him about my observance about him so far.

Feeling hesitant I asked him, why do you look so pale, why your music has deep grief and hidden meaning? Is it by choice or your life is a turmoil of bad incidences which you are releasing through music. Thankfully he got opened up, maybe when I told him that I'm an author and your secrets will be only in words without knowing the source. He laughed and continued…

He narrated;

Quite well I knew her, and ours was a beautiful relationship. There was nothing impossible between us. We fall in love and got married. I proposed her at our first sight. She was different from me. There were many things that did not match between us. She was strong and beautiful women. A perfect example of bold and beautiful. Everything was going smooth for me, but maybe not for her. One day we both realised that there is some bitterness added to our relationship. The silence between us grew.

We started to quarrel and were not on terms most of the time. I would not say that it was only her fault but I could not gauge what is happening. I was naïve and stupid for not understanding her dreams and aspirations. She was different. Her light reflected abundance of love and compassion. Today I realise that it was my ego I think that made her go.

Soreness surrounded us when I saw her getting attracted to another man. He happens to be my best friend. She became close to him and our distress intensified. She found solace and a friend in him which went missing in us. Slowly my world started to fall apart and they both grew closer. I started feeling angry and filled with anguish for my friend. I used to think that at least he could have stopped her from being close to him.

My anger led me to do things that took her to depression. Without understanding what she might have been going through and what actually is the reason for her to get into this relationship I kept on abusing and thrashing her with abusive words. My life turned upside down with these incidences.

Few months passed and she even tried to explain to me about her relationship and why and what all she is going through and what is the real reason for her closeness to his friend. Time stood still for both of us. But we were not the only ones who suffered. My friend was married too and when his wife came to know about this relationship, she also could not take it.

My friend's wife belonged to a village hence for her it was tougher to smell the sight of a new relationship which she angrily took as cheating. Time passed in this compulsive relationship between us and took us apart light years. It was inseparable and unbreakable. I was no more friends with my best buddy.

I repeatedly took her for granted and she kept on trying hard to make me understand and feel contented on what has happened is not cheating; but side effects of grouchy relationship. We both lived in this impelling relationship for a long until she broke deep into her depression and was almost to finish her life. Then she went numb forever….

She left me forever, from where I can't even think of pulling her back. The deep guilt in me for not giving her a possibility to amend, remained in my heart. She collapsed due to a mental stroke and could not take on life. Now when I have lost her for ever I feel, I kept dragging my ego to heights and she left me behind with all my sins alone.

My regrets keep eating me and time has frozen forever. With pain, now I know that I could have stopped her going so deep in depression. Or even could have tried to mend things between us. Not thrashing her all the time, since, for what happened was not in her hand neither it was in mine.

Guilt – Right or Wrong?

Today I'm a successful musician, kept lingering to the thought that my mistakes and my attitude towards life, took everything of mine. Still keep lurking on those incidences when she would come and plead me for forgiveness or would apologise knowing that she is not completely wrong or she would come and persuade me to communicate, but now it is just darkness.

Did I give up to life or took a life away?

Let It Go!

No one is perfect. No one does everything right all the time. Especially when you feel guilty about something which you have done or not done you relate it with time situations and your conscience. But in actual it is about your consciousness. When you act on something, you do not think it is right or wrong, you just act. Guilt will try to control your emotions. Do not let it do this with you. Lead with your consciousness inclusivity. When in a toxic relationship, or dealing shame, do this with your creativity not with your social conscience. Ideally, it is like you know that this will not work for me, so you would be reluctant to work this way for hours as well. In this situation, the relationship goes for a toss. *That's all it is.*

Just try to fix things with universal consciousness, not with your current emotion. For example, even a criminal would think that killing this person is right because he is a rival and causing harm to his success. Whatever the reason may be for this person, killing is not right. Now, who will decide what is right or wrong? Everyone does things without thinking right or wrong

Guilt – Right or Wrong?

and they feel they are doing the right thing. In life, the real question is that whether these actions are necessary or not or what and how they will impact our lives. *It is not about shame or guilt or right or wrong.*

Let go of all the shame and guilt in you. Live life with humanity and joyfulness, this will bring you close to your true nature, when this will happen you would be known beforehand that what is right or wrong and you could act accordingly. This will make your relationships harmonious.

An Apology To My Future Self

Letting go of past regrets is not easy. It is chained to the deepest consciousness. When referring to past mistakes, you may feel embarrassed about your actions. Forgiving yourself is easy to say, but the toughest part to execute. As, we humans mess up all the time and then get shame, humiliation, and self-condemnation. We all have been there in these situations. But admitting that you are in a mess ease out the pain and shame to some extent.

At times, forgiving yourself is not that difficult it may sound. How?

Express your sorry to your friend whom you may have hurt.

You can just go and apologize.

Or you have yelled at your kid in your mood swings. You can apologise, say, "I'm sorry".

On the other hand, it is not easy to forgive yourself or apologize for your actions, when you have completely ignored a homeless person who needed your help or

Guilt – Right or Wrong?

you have ignored a kid who needed urgent help. You can't amend it, because chances to meet these people again in life are rare.

So if self-forgiveness is this easy why we can't get over it and keep getting tangled in the shadow of guilt. Is it because we are chained to our past? Also whenever you get stuck in a situation or when you are feeling sorry for yourself, just think that what is the point of feeling apologetic of something you can't change in past.

Like, one of my friend who is an interior designer and a single mom. One fine night, her son came to her and asked her to sleep with him. She sweetly replied and said No, as she was tired and had a very big pitch presentation next morning. He requested once again and said mom for five minutes sleep with me then you work. She wanted but she can't as next day was a big day for her and have to be upright. She said love you will be fine, please go and sleep, will come in some time.

The night passed, and the next day while returning from school, he met with an accident and dies on the spot. The only motive to infer this incidence is that time is in no one's control. For her whole life, she cursed herself for what happened to her only child. She was all alone and regretted not being with him that night. I want to

Guilt – Right or Wrong?

highlight one thing, in this story, when you do not know what will happen in the future and can't change it, then how could you change the past either. As its said work on your present so your past becomes good and future better.

People would remind her of all the things she had done for her son and the wonderful life and love he was given, but it wasn't enough for her. She constantly questioned why I hadn't done more.

After a few years, she realized that guilt was consuming her and in order for her to move on, she needed to find a way to let go and forgive herself.

She was weighed down because she was living a life consumed by the past. Guilt did not allow her to be fully present with her family, or to see all the good that she had in her life then and now.

She had to accept that no matter what she could never change her past, but she could change the way she remembered her precious time with her son. Once she did, she was able to free herself from the feeling of being the victim of the time.

Guilt is an absurd emotion that is complex and can't be tackled with one solution. There are different means

Guilt – Right or Wrong?

which can help you let go of the guilt and empty your mind from the mess that is being created due to an action of yours which can only be corrected and not reversed what so ever.

∞∞∞∞∞∞∞∞∞∞∞∞∞∞∞∞∞∞∞∞∞∞∞∞∞∞∞∞∞∞∞∞

Guilt – Right or Wrong?

New Baby – New Life

I've been with my husband for 10 years now. We have a 3-year-old son. Soon after having my son, I have apprehended just how toxic my husband is. We have spent months quarrelling and I have been belligerent and fighting for this relationship. And I have seen some immediate and noticeable changes in him, though maybe, he is trying. But I am still finding myself stung by him more than I deserve, and I also have conviction that his conduct and lack of emotional support and caring, has made me fall out of love with him.

I mean, is that even feasible? I don't want to fall out of love with him, I was once so much in love with him that it was appalling. Now I can't stand the thought of him even touching me. But I don't want that. I want us to be close and work on our connection with ourselves and our son. And I want our marriage that I daydreamed of being as beautiful as it was earlier. He is the man I saw myself being with forever till my last breath, but now I feel so diverged and muddled and hurt. I really don't know what to do.

Guilt – Right or Wrong?

A new baby in your family calls for a lot of changes in relationships between husband and wife and among other family members. What you are expressing is understandable. The important question to be asked is, were these problems have always been there? Or it started popping-up since son arrived in our lives?

It became tough for her to recall good times spent with her husband. Do you remember a time when your husband gave you the emotional support you needed? And if things have got worse since the birth of your son, then it's conceivable that your husband just doesn't know how to react to these new changes, or what to do to give his wife what she need. It can be a confusing time for everyone including him.

New babies are a gorgeous addition to any family, but they can unquestionably put a pressure on the relationship for a while, at least until everyone has attuned to the new normal. If you can remember a time you and your husband were close and loving and nurturing, keep fighting for the relationship to bring it on the track. It's so important to have time out with just the two of you, if you can to relink and rekindle the emotional well-being in your marriage. It's important to

Guilt – Right or Wrong?

be able to reconnect as a couple sometimes. This will be important for your son too.

If you can, and if you aren't doing this already, it might also be helpful if your husband can have time on his own with his son while you do something that feels nurturing for you – whether it's having a quick catch up with friends, having asleep! going to a movie. Sometimes new dads struggle with where they fit in, as their new role in the family when a baby arrives. It is the time, just for your husband and your son to build their bond and connect as father and son might help this situation to ease.

∞∞∞∞∞∞∞∞∞∞∞∞∞∞∞∞∞∞∞∞∞∞∞∞∞∞∞∞∞∞∞∞

Resilience Is The Antidote To Shame And Guilt In Teens

Needless to say, teenage is the most dangerous growth years in the 21st century. On the contrary, it is one of the most delicate and easy to shape phases of human life. Whether you are a teen of the 21st century or way back times, the trauma which a child faces in the early years, stay with him/her lifelong. Resilience is one major factor to create embarrassment during these times.

Many emotions in teens cultivate during the development of their self-years. Some fight with a loss of confidence, some with shame and others with awkward moments. There is much research to back this that teens face devastating issues in their age when they start associating themselves with others. In this scenario, they sometimes feel ashamed of themselves for not achieving or having certain benefits which their fellow mates have. They also start feeling self-resilient towards their own life situations. This heightens sensitivity towards other's opinions on them.

Guilt – Right or Wrong?

Eventually, embarrassment and shame become home in their pool of emotions. With this they feel they must have done something wrong or did wrong thus, they are treated like this.

The positive side to this factor is that if adolescents face guilty situations their conscience knows how to deal with it. Maybe not diplomatically as we adults do, but they know this action will make this right.

For example; a teen brought to London but have Indian values. She is a brat by her choices and does not fall under the category of social values and stigmas. On the other hand, the family is typical Indian, despite the fact living in London for years and have no plans to return too. She has compulsive behaviour and no anger management in her life. The kid who is in high school and being treated bad or bullied for her brown skin was traumatising to her.

When Margret watches her multilingual friends from different countries been mellowed with each other, she feels disappointed of not being in their group and why she is the one who is not treated great in school and around. She used to think maybe the brown colour is the problem. Foolishly she tried putting shabby makeup to become white and dress like them to be among them to get acceptance. She failed, rather she becomes a laughing cow in front of the whole school. Her embarrassment was rising immensely. The guy who used to bully and make fun of her all the time, in her adolescent mind she thought to teach a lesson to him. She lied to his girlfriend about him cheating on her. She also secretly dogged handwriting and wrote seducing message to another girl to show his girlfriend that he is cheating on you. When his girlfriend came to know about all this, she got furious and broke up with him. They were madly into each other and kind of serious boyfriend and girlfriend (you know how teen love affairs are). But cheating, lying, forging handwriting is not right to act to perform.

Margret knows it all. Still, she did as the embarrassment and disgrace reached the pinnacle. Initially, for a few days, she thought that doing this to that guy who bullied her will make her feel happy and will release her from her racial trauma situations. But nothing of this sort happened and she was futile again.

Few days passed…during dinner time, her mom was discussing something about her work with Margret's father. She was sharing how one manager troubles her all the time and do not give credit to her for her work. He even complained falsely to the director about Margret's mom. This is making me uncomfortable and may hamper my promotion. I feel like complaining too about him to everyone in the office. Margret's father, on the other hand, denied doing so and told her mother that if you become the way people are with you then the same thing will repeat and repeat and nothing will change in you. If they are bad let them be, you can't change them, but you change yourself by not responding to their bad actions. Watching them talk, she understood that what she did was wrong and immediately guilt took all over her.

Here, with her conscience saying that she did wrong, she would amend it, as teens in their behaviour are fragile and they overcome guilt easily and correct it too. As I mentioned that they are hugely sensitive towards other's opinions, which sometimes goes in their favour to become good. Margret took it the same way and apologised for what she did, yes it wasn't easy at all. But her conscience values made her do the right actions and she made her life easy and sorted. *The antidote to guilt is conscience, which she used and she was able to come out from her guilt.*

Guilt – Right or Wrong?

For teens and adolescents' trauma affects their brain. They are exposed to adverse childhood experiences (ACE's). Due to which they can experience shame, guilt, embarrassment quite often. Usually, shame is a different emotion that is not directly termed similar to guilt. Guilt is usually an outward behaviour that results from the shame that is deep-rooted in our belief system. Now when a teen's mind, experiences humiliation, disgrace, trauma, disapproval etc., the belief system gets shaken up. Later which may result in some actions by the child that may result in guilt.

Let's see another piece from a small place in India, where a teen (Naina) got molested by her uncle.

In a country where superstitions related to girl children and boy children are widespread, this act was not at all graceful. When she got sexually molested by her uncle, emotion which she created was trauma, self-resilience, shame, fear, etc. As a teen, she wasn't able to convey all this to her mom or anyone else in the family, as these emotions were overpowering her. Moreover, the symptoms and consequences of molestation are not registered in her conscience, except that this touch is not all good. There are billions of these examples like Naina those who experience such abuse and live with it whole life. But the feeling of pain, trauma and shame does not leave them. Research shows that teens who experience sexual abuse in their teen life, are more likely to indulge in multiple sex partners when they become adults. They may engage in risky behaviours which is a direct result of the trauma they faced.

They may also indulge in drugs/alcohol and are prone to get sexually transmitted diseases. For them, these actions may be normal but they are the reactions of shame and trauma they felt in teens. These abnormal circumstances are directly related to their past embarrassment which then result in guilt. These behaviour in adulthood create problems to deal with people. They may do a lot of self-talk, they may become self-resilient, or they may also start developing an "I'm bad attitude". To condemn this behaviour they may indulge in creating a "fake-self". This belief perpetuates the feeling of indignity even more eventually with moral and social guilt. Do remember that chronic feelings of dishonour can lead to self-loathing and social withdrawal.

Let It Go!

Shame and resilience are two emotions that are directly connected with our inner guilt. In these scenarios, the most crucial part is "not to judge". For example, if you put to shame and guilt in a petri dish it will need three things to grow exponentially: secrecy, silence, and judgement. It is important to note that instead of asking a question "what's wrong with you? ask how can I help you? Or "what happened to you".

One thing we all shall know when dealing with teens on their guilt and shame is always try to understand the underlying thought behind their actions. Try to know what are the contributing factors behind their acts. For example, a normal reaction to sexual abuse trauma experienced in the past can lead to increase sexual behaviour as a way of connecting with others, or essentially, seeking love. Negatively judging a teen for their behaviour will hinder one's ability to support them. If we can let go of the need to control their behaviour and instead approach them with compassion and empathy, they are more likely to feel cared for and understood. The basis for feeling loved and having a sense of belonging is when a person feels understood. This is often what hurting adolescents are searching for through their risky behaviours.

One of the best ways to deal with teen guilt is to be with them and take life their way. Communicate and spend time. Try to inculcate the feeling of empathy in them. Empathy and sympathy are two different things thus, make sure you are not persistent in sympathy as in severe cases, you would have to go to the therapist too. Engage in creative stuff with them as their mind will be conditioned in some constructive actions.

∞∞∞∞∞∞∞∞∞∞∞∞∞∞∞∞∞∞∞∞∞∞∞∞∞∞∞∞∞∞∞∞∞∞∞

Guilt – Right or Wrong?

"Set a clock timer and let your rivulet of consciousness ooze out onto the paper."

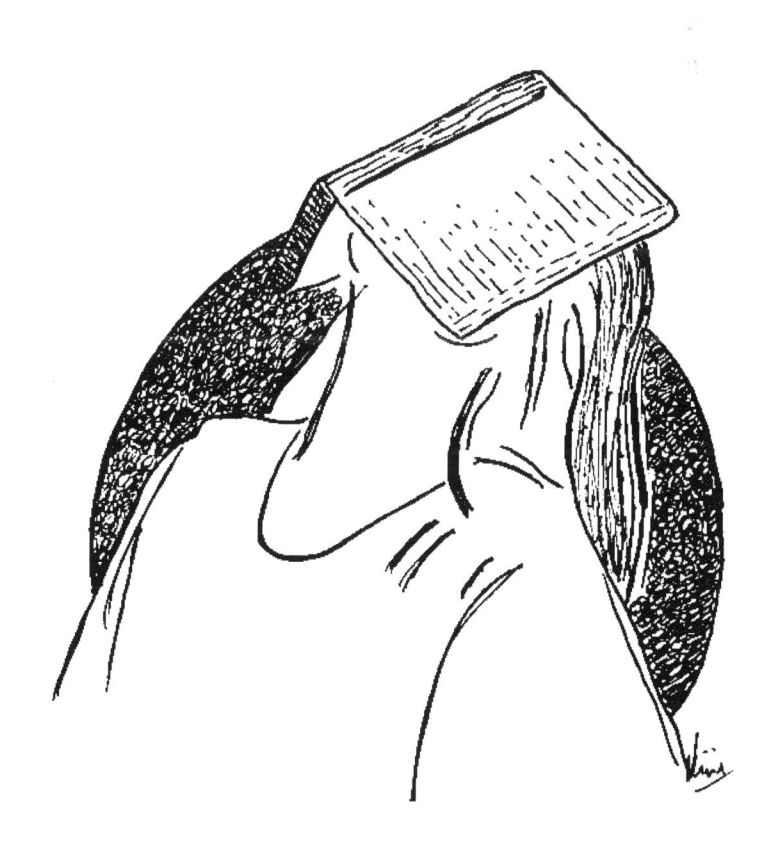

Heal Yourself – Test Yourself

Journal writing for evaluating guilt and other factors that related to regrets.

Emotions like shame, apology, embarrassment are directly linked with the emotion of guilt. Guilt and shame are deep-seated emotions that have a strong back on our past memories. Try to be honest with yourself and write it down what you feel about it.

Let's start:

If I perform an action that created a fuss around me and I keep on thinking about it all the time without doing anything about it. *(if your answer is a "YES" then "why")*

_____

_____

Guilt – Right or Wrong?

When I do something wrong and I know about it, I get anxiety feeling. (if your answer is a "YES" then "why")

_____

_____

I feel guilty most of the time even though I have no idea from where it is coming from. (if your answer is a "YES" then "why")

_____

_____

I'm losing hope that I will never be a good person in my life again. (if your answer is a "YES" then "why")

_____

_____

Guilt – Right or Wrong?

I blame myself for things and actions that other people do not think of me or care about me. (if your answer is a "YES" then "why")

_____

_____

I get sunk in me at times, without a reason and get lost in my own world. (if your answer is a "YES" then "why")

_____

_____

I experience moments when I can't even look up to myself in the mirror, without understanding or knowing the exact reason. (if your answer is a "YES" then "why")

_____

_____

Guilt – Right or Wrong?

I experience moments when everything said and done by others affect me. (if your answer is a "YES" then "why")

_____

_____

I feel the need to explain or apologise for the reasons for my actions or behaviour to others. (if your answer is a "YES" then "why")

_____

_____

I feel embarrassed about dodging my friend over another without any reason. (if your answer is a "YES" then "why")

_____

_____

Assess Your Guilt Quotient

Assess yourself with these actions or things which you invariably do sometimes. These incidences are day-to-day and you would relate. The practice is the same, keep yourself in that situation and choose the best option. This will help you in assessing your guilt emotion and other sentiments associated with it in given situations.

Guilt – Right or Wrong?

Let's start:

You are walking in the middle of a busy street. You stumble on the ground. All your books and pens fall out of your bag on the street. While thinking about it later the day, what would you feel?

Would you feel shame/embarrassed?

Would you feel anxious?

Next time will you be confident in your actions ignoring the past

You will be guilty of your action thinking you are hopeless

Guilt – Right or Wrong?

You get a very bad grade at school. You got scolding from your parents. Your best friends in the group all scored great credits. Later in the night, you were thinking about those bad grades, what would you feel?

Would you feel shame/embarrassed?

Would you feel anxious?

Next time will you be confident in your actions ignoring the past

You will be guilty of your action thinking you are hopeless

You are going to your school. In fun/agitation you have cut your own hair and now you feel stupid on how fellow mates would look at you. How would you feel?

Would you feel shame/embarrassed?

Would you feel anxiety?

Next time will you be confident in your actions ignoring the past.

You will be guilty of your action thinking you are hopeless.

Guilt – Right or Wrong?

You are riding a bike onto the pavement. You dashed a stone and tumbled. People stop to watch. Some are laughing and some show support. You left quickly. While thinking about it later how would you feel?

Would you feel shame/embarrassed?

Would you feel anxious?

Next time will you be confident in your actions ignoring the past.

You will be guilty of your action thinking you are hopeless.

You are standing in front of the class. You have to give a presentation. Everyone is looking at you. You forget what you wanted to say and you froze due to nervousness. What would you feel later that evening about this incidence?

Would you feel shame/embarrassed?

Would you feel anxious?

Next time will you be confident in your actions ignoring the past

You will be guilty of your action thinking you are hopeless

Guilt – Right or Wrong?

You are at your peer's house for the first time. You get a glass of chocolate milk. Glassed slipped from your hand and milk spilled on the carpet. Oops. How would you feel once back home?

Would you feel shame/embarrassed?

Would you feel anxious?

Next time will you be confident in your actions ignoring the past

You will be guilty of your action thinking you are hopeless

Your fellow student is using the red pen the whole time. You also need a pen. You snatch away the pen just like that. Classmate broke up with you and tension aroused between you two. How would feel about the friendship in later days?

Would you feel shame/embarrassed?

Would you feel anxious?

Next time will you be confident in your actions ignoring the past

You will be guilty of your action thinking you are hopeless

Guilt – Right or Wrong?

In the middle of the night you are driving back home. You are going super-fast. Suddenly you saw a little girl standing near to the pavement and you bump into her. How would you feel about this incidence later?

Would you feel shame/embarrassed?

Would you feel anxious?

Next time will you be confident in your actions ignoring the past

You will be guilty of your action thinking you are hopeless

You want to go home quickly. One little girl from next door drops her marbles on the ground. You don't help her, because you're in a hurry. How would feel about your behaviour towards the child later on?

Would you feel shame/embarrassed?

Would you feel anxious?

You will be guilty of your action thinking you are hopeless

Guilt – Right or Wrong?

Your mom worked a long time on a painting. But you don't watch out. You knock over a glass of water on her drawing. Everything spills over the painting. The painting is ruined. She was upset, how would you feel?

Would you feel shame/embarrassed?

Would you feel anxiety?

Next time will you be confident in your actions ignoring the past

You will be guilty of your action thinking you are hopeless

Your classmate hasn't finished her essay on time. She asks you for your help. You don't help her, because you don't feel like it. And she failed the essay competition. How would you feel next day to school on knowing her result?

Would you feel shame/embarrassed?

Would you feel anxious?

Next time will you be confident in your actions ignoring the past

You will be guilty of your action thinking you are hopeless

Assessment

PS: if your maximum answers of yours are: *Would you feel anxious?*

Then you shall not worry as it is the instant reaction to any action which is unforeseen or not in your control.

If your maximum answers are: *Would you feel shame/embarrassed?*

You shall watch out your actions in future, because if this repeats with every action of yours and becoming a habit then it may worsen and take charge to severe guilt and distress.

If your maximum answers are: *You will be guilty of your action thinking you are hopeless*

This is serious, as guilt has already trapped you. Working on it becomes prudent. Use the "let it go" sections of this book and overcome it.

Guilt – Right or Wrong?

If your maximum answers are: *Next time will you be confident in your actions ignoring the past*

It is of course a healthy sign. You are watchful, mindful of your actions and make deliberate attempt to be vigilant.

∞∞∞∞∞∞∞∞∞∞∞∞∞∞∞∞∞∞∞∞∞∞∞∞∞∞∞∞∞∞

Guilt – Right or Wrong?

Talk To Yourself

Let's ask some questions to ourselves about guilt and the emotions related to it. By far you all must be knowing the complexity of this emotion. It arises from within and we have the power to fix it. Interrogating ourselves is the best way to understand how much you feel guilt-ridden about things you perform on daily life and of course the acts of past that keep us trapped in our guilt.

1. Have you used guilt as a tool with others to try to get what you want? If yes, How?

_____

_____

_____

_____

Guilt – Right or Wrong?

_____

_____

_____

2. What is that one act or incidence you did when on high with some substance or drug or alcohol? Do you feel guilty about it today and also feel horrible about your toxic substance use?

_____

_____

_____

_____

_____

_____

Guilt – Right or Wrong?

3. When was the last time that you can remember lying to someone, which changed the whole career of that person for all wrong reasons and got into a huge problem. Do you feel guilty about it?

_____

_____

_____

_____

_____

_____

_____

_____

4. When is the last time you let someone down? How do you feel about it now?

_____

_____

_____

5. When is the last time you felt embarrassment (like a bad person for some reason)?

6. Do you ever feel like a "immoral" parent, spouse, or child?

_____

_____

_____

_____

_____

_____

_____

_____

7. What is one of the worst things that you have ever done that you can still remember?

_____

_____

_____

_____

8. What do you feel, remorse, shame or proud about, when it comes to your family?

Guilt – Right or Wrong?

9. Did you ever intentionally miffed someone?

___

10. Do you think that you have a problem dealing with guilt? If so, how do you know about it? Have you ever thought of tackling it?

Guilt – Right or Wrong?

_____

_____

_____

_____

_____

_____

11. Do you ever feel like you should have been there for someone but you weren't?

_____

_____

_____

_____

_____

_____

_____

Guilt – Right or Wrong?

12. What is something that you got away with easily, and you know it is wrong, but you have guilt about it?

_____

_____

_____

_____

_____

_____

_____

_____

_____

_____

13. Have you ever gone out of your way to try to make someone else feel guilty, just to justify your anger, ego or take revenge?

_____

_____

_____

_____

_____

_____

_____

_____

14. How do other people use "guilt trips" to manipulate you?

_____

_____

Guilt – Right or Wrong?

_____

_____

_____

_____

_____

_____

15. Do you ever feel guilty that you do not spend enough quality time with someone?

_____

_____

_____

_____

_____

_____

_____

_____

Guilt – Right or Wrong?

16. What is one thing that comes to mind right now that you are sorry for?

_____

_____

_____

_____

_____

_____

_____

_____

_____

17. Do you feel any stress or guilt about the way that you have spoken to someone recently?

_____

_____

Guilt – Right or Wrong?

_____

_____

_____

_____

_____

_____

_____

18. What is one thing that you can think of, which you have done in past and you are aware of the act. You know that maybe you should feel guilty about it, but you don't?

_____

_____

_____

_____

_____

Guilt – Right or Wrong?

_____

_____

_____

_____

19. What have you done to make compensation to someone you have victimized or wounded?

_____

_____

_____

_____

_____

_____

_____

_____

Guilt – Right or Wrong?

20. Who would you most need forgiveness from today and why?

_____

_____

_____

_____

_____

_____

_____

_____

21. Do you ever feel guilty when you are not supposed to?

_____

_____

_____

Guilt – Right or Wrong?

22. What is one of the nastiest things that you ever got caught doing or trying to do?

Guilt – Right or Wrong?

23. Describe circumstances you used to feel guilt or disgrace about, but now that weight has been lifted from you.

_____

_____

_____

_____

_____

_____

_____

_____

_____

_____

24. Is there anything that you are having trouble forgiving someone else for?

_____

_____

_____

_____

_____

_____

_____

_____

_____

25. Is there anything that you are having trouble pardoning yourself for?

_____

_____

Guilt – Right or Wrong?

_____

_____

_____

_____

_____

_____

_____

_____

26. Is there anything that your parents said or did to you when you were growing and you still feel the pain?

_____

_____

_____

_____

_____

Guilt – Right or Wrong?

27. What destructive messages do you ask or say sometimes to yourself, especially, when you feel evil?

Because this topic is challenging, I'm ending this journal writing with Questions 28, 29 And 30 for you to analyse the real you and know yourself better. It will also lead you towards Positivity.

28. What is one thing that you have changed or done for the betterment of your life?

_____

_____

_____

_____

_____

_____

_____

_____

Guilt – Right or Wrong?

29. What is that one thing that you can think of that you have done to help someone who is in need?

_____

_____

_____

_____

_____

_____

_____

_____

_____

_____

_____

30. What is that thing in your life right now that you feel grateful about, in present?

_____

_____

_____

_____

_____

_____

_____

_____

_____

_____

_____

∞∞∞∞∞∞∞∞∞∞∞∞∞∞∞∞∞∞∞∞∞∞∞∞∞∞∞∞∞∞∞∞∞

Guilt Proneness Scale

Guilt Proneness scale – let's do this and know our selves for our own betterment. While attempting this, make sure you keep yourself in that situation and then think how would react or feel or act later, once the moment has passed, as guilt emerge a bit later when the incidence of action is done.

PS: These are real-life situations from real people which we all encounter in day-to-day life. You need to imagine yourself in the situation and then select the best fit option for you.

Guilt – Right or Wrong?

Let me share an example with you for a clearer understanding.

You have made plans for dinner with your girlfriend. You realized at 10 that you didn't show up to her.

- You can't apologise enough for forgetting the most important dinner (it is ruminative guilt)
- You would think I'm inconsistent towards her (feeling of shame)
- You would think, well she would understand, it is not a big deal. (detachment)
- You would think to try to make it up to her as soon as possible. (non-ruminative guilt)

While attempting these you would see that you may fall for one of those options. This would make you understand how much prone are you to guilt or how many times you feel shame or get embarrassed about the actions you performed or you are just ignorant. You can choose one out of four.

SCORING: The scale is scored by averaging all items. Higher scores indicate more guilt-proneness for you in a given circumstance.

Guilt – Right or Wrong?

Let's start with the process of knowing yourself even better.

— You are at store: After realizing you have received extra change at a store from the storekeeper, you decide to keep it because the cash counter guys aren't noticing? What is the likelihood of feeling at that moment for not keeping the money?

Extremely Unlikely

Unlikely

Likely Extremely

Likely

— You secretly commit a crime. What is the likelihood that you would feel remorse about breaking the law in later days?

Extremely Unlikely

Unlikely

Likely Extremely

Likely

Guilt – Right or Wrong?

— At a superior housewarming party, you spill red wine on their new peach-coloured mosaic carpet. You cover the stain with a corner chest so that nobody notices your mess. What is the likelihood that you would feel that the way you acted as wretched after a few days?

Extremely Unlikely

Unlikely

Likely Extremely

Likely

— You lie to people but they never find out about it. What is the likelihood that you would feel terrible about the lies you told?

Extremely Unlikely

Unlikely

Likely Extremely

Likely

Guilt – Right or Wrong?

— Out of frustration, you break the printer machine at work. Nobody is around you and you leave without telling anyone. What is the likelihood you would feel bad about the way you acted after a few days?

Extremely Unlikely

Unlikely

Likely Extremely

Likely

— You are privately informed that you are the only one in your group in the high school who hasn't made it through the finals grade assessment as you skipped too many days of school. What is the likelihood that this would lead you to become more responsible about attending school in the coming months?

Extremely Unlikely

Unlikely

Likely Extremely

Likely

Guilt – Right or Wrong?

— You tore a page of the article out of a journal from the library and take it with you. Your teacher notices the event and tells the librarian and your entire class. What is the likelihood that this would make you feel like a bad person when you later realise what you did?

Extremely Unlikely

Unlikely

Likely Extremely

Likely

— After making a big blunder in a project at work in which huge business gimmicks was involved, your boss condemns you in front of your co-workers. What is the likelihood that you would fake the condition and leave work in the coming months?

Extremely Unlikely

Unlikely

Likely Extremely

Likely

Guilt – Right or Wrong?

— You reveal your best friend's secret, although your friend never finds out. But what is the likelihood that your failure to keep the secret would lead you to wield extra effort to keep secrets in the future?

Extremely Unlikely

Unlikely

Likely Extremely

Likely

— You give a ruthless presentation at work. Afterwards, your boss tells you to visit (www.xyz.com) for more self-assessments, self-improvement. And your fellow mates blamed you for losing the contract. What is the likelihood that you would feel hopeless about it, then and later?

Extremely Unlikely

Unlikely

Likely Extremely

Likely

Guilt – Right or Wrong?

— A friend tells you that you hype that deal. What is the likelihood that you would stop spending time with that friend in future?

Extremely Unlikely

Unlikely

Likely Extremely

Likely

— Your home is very chaotic and unexpected guests knock on your door and invite themselves in. What is the likelihood that you would avoid the guests until they leave?

Extremely Unlikely

Unlikely

Likely Extremely

Likely

Guilt – Right or Wrong?

— You effectively embellish your damages in a lawsuit. Months later, your lies are exposed and you are charged with untruthfulness. What is the likelihood that you would think you are a dreadful human being of what you did?

Extremely Unlikely

Unlikely

Likely Extremely

Likely

— You powerfully defend an opinion in a discussion taking place, and though nobody was conscious of it, then you realize that you were wrong. What is the likelihood that this would make you think more carefully before you speak in future among people?

Extremely Unlikely

Unlikely

Likely Extremely

Likely

Guilt – Right or Wrong?

— You take office materials home for personal use and then are caught by your manager. What is the likelihood that this would lead you to quit your job in the coming days or months?

Extremely Unlikely

Unlikely

Likely Extremely

Likely

— You make a fault at work and find out that your fellow mate is blamed for your error. Later, when he confronts you about your mistake. What is the likelihood that you would feel apologetic?

Extremely Unlikely

Unlikely

Likely Extremely

Likely

Guilt – Right or Wrong?

— While debating a frenzied subject with friends, you abruptly realize you are shouting though nobody seems to notice. What is the likelihood that you would try to act more considerate toward your friend next time?

Extremely Unlikely

Unlikely

Likely Extremely

Likely

— You are taking care of a dog of your friend, while your friend is on a vacation. Would you feel terrible and incompetent for not being able to handle the dog properly?

Extremely Unlikely

Unlikely

Likely Extremely

Likely

Guilt – Right or Wrong?

Remember guilt self-talk is good. And if your answers are matching with guilt self-talk and falling in the scale of Extremely likely - where you are likely to take corrective action then you can lead your life guilt-free.

Journal Prompt For Manifestation

Some quick journal prompts which you shall do for your happy life. If you write it down daily like you manifest your dreams, you would for sure get out of any negative, shameful or guilt-ridden memories of your past or present. These are few, likewise, you can make your prompts daily and just write them out or you can catch me on Instagram @authorontravel for help, assistance, counsel.

It is your safe personal space. Give it a shot!

What is your first memory of guilt?

_____

_____

_____

_____

Guilt – Right or Wrong?

_____

_____

_____

_____

What other memories do you have of regrets?

_____

_____

_____

_____

_____

_____

_____

Guilt – Right or Wrong?

What did you feel regret about your present-day?

_____

_____

_____

_____

_____

_____

_____

Do you feel guilt-ridden about small things?

_____

_____

_____

_____

_____

Guilt – Right or Wrong?

_____

_____

_____

When you get a feeling of regret what do you do? You hide, you get angry, you blame someone else.

_____

_____

_____

_____

_____

_____

_____

Guilt – Right or Wrong?

Are you around people who make you feel guilty?

_____

_____

_____

_____

_____

_____

_____

_____

When did you start feeling remorse for something you did in the past?

_____

_____

_____

_____

Guilt – Right or Wrong?

_____

_____

_____

_____

How often do you trace those feelings in you? (continued from above question)

_____

_____

_____

_____

_____

_____

_____

_____

Guilt – Right or Wrong?

Does your job give you some sort of guilt?

_____

_____

_____

_____

_____

_____

_____

Write down 5 stressors that give you the feeling of shame.

_____

_____

_____

_____

Guilt – Right or Wrong?

_____

_____

_____

_____

_____

Write five things which you think you did wrong and have regrets about them.

_____

_____

_____

_____

_____

_____

_____

Guilt – Right or Wrong?

Find out 5 names around you who does not exist for you for real, still, you have to be with them.

_____

_____

_____

_____

_____

_____

_____

_____

When was the last time you were compassionate to yourself?

_____

_____

_____

Guilt – Right or Wrong?

___

___

___

___

___

___

When is the last time you loved yourself?

___

___

___

___

___

___

___

Guilt – Right or Wrong?

Write down 3 things in which way you can constructively use your guilt.

_____

_____

_____

_____

_____

_____

_____

_____

Write down that one thing which is holding you back from moving on? And what you can do to get it removed from your life?

_____

_____

Guilt – Right or Wrong?

_____

_____

_____

_____

_____

_____

_____

Write down the origin of your guilt, like is it from the past, is it from an external source or it is from within.

_____

_____

_____

_____

_____

_____

Guilt – Right or Wrong?

_____

_____

_____

_____

Write down how social media give you guilt.

_____

_____

_____

_____

_____

_____

_____

_____

Guilt – Right or Wrong?

If you think that your guilt is irrational then write it down how you are healing and can forgive yourself.

_____

_____

_____

_____

_____

_____

_____

_____

_____

What are the things that are not going well in your life?

_____

_____

Guilt – Right or Wrong?

Journal Prompts For Vivid Moods

When in Stress, give it a try.

Think about liberation: Think about life: Think about mindfulness: how does it show up for you? Describe the vibrations, the opinions, the perceptions, the way your mind and body feel when you experience stress. Maybe it's the respite of sending an email you've obligatory to send, or maybe it's the relief of getting some noble news about an adored one's health. Explore everything, describe it in detail, welcome it, do not fear.

_____

_____

_____

_____

_____

_____

Guilt – Right or Wrong?

_____

_____

_____

_____

_____

_____

_____

When in Ambiguity or Uncertainty, speak out.

When it doubts, go memory lane. When full of doubt, not sure where to go next? Concentrate your thoughts from younger version of yourself. What does the 16-year-old version of you looked like or would think of where you're at? Ask in those thoughts, for an opinion. You may not come up with an answer, but it'll get you thinking about a problem that you are facing right now from a new perspective. Write it down!

Guilt – Right or Wrong?

Guilt – Right or Wrong?

Self-Loathing is harmful, let it go.

COVID-19 has made the world stand still, and for those who are working relentlessly from home during lockdowns for the first time in life, for them life is daunting. Amidst this the Google meets, Zoom calls have made you put in front of people the you've never experienced before. Because of this if you're feeling self-critical, write a list of things you like about your appearance, dressing, hair style, overall look etc.

If you'd rather not concentrate on your appearance, then ask yourself: What are the words you would love to hear from someone you trust? Or What are those words you wish others shall say about you. Become that person. Write it down. Be specific, direct, unabashed.

_____

_____

_____

_____

_____

_____

Guilt – Right or Wrong?

_____

_____

_____

_____

_____

_____

_____

_____

Practice APATHY, but be careful...

Kudos for identifying that this is what you're feeling at the moment. As many does not recognise it happening or do not consider it as an important feeling. In a world where you "feel everything" you feel lethargy as well. You don't have to force any emotion on you; you can take rest too.

Spend some time resting, thinking, just maybe doing nothing. List out ways you've helped others. Then, ask

Guilt – Right or Wrong?

yourself: how are you helping others, now? Or, how are your skills distinctively placed to make the world a better place? Connect the dots between what you are adept of and what the world needs. Write it down!

_____

_____

_____

_____

_____

_____

_____

_____

_____

Guilt – Right or Wrong?

Loneliness or Seclusion – this is dangerous, speak out.

If you're not able to be with a person who make you feel loved and being attended, then write an entry in your journal about the moments of warmth and embrace. What greetings have you received from them? Or from strangers? How your closest friends describe you to their friends, family and relatives?

If it is challenging to find friendliness from others to call upon, please know, that's okay. Instead, call upon the things that assist you, the ground beneath your feet, the air you breathe, the plants around you, the breath supporting your body, the water you drink, the tap water you use. Then, jump into making some self-validating notes: for example, I trust myself, I love myself, I belong here, this is my world, I am good, I'm in safe hands. For all intents and purposes, you will write yourself a love note in kind and affirming language.

_____

_____

_____

Guilt – Right or Wrong?

_____

_____

_____

_____

_____

_____

_____

_____

_____

_____

Fear, Panic – takes you away from real meaning of life. Take action on them.

Raise your hand if you don't feel anxiety about what's happening in the world or around you. No raised hands? Okay. Now, grab your journal and ask yourself: How have others presented you generosity or generous

Guilt – Right or Wrong?

acts? And how can you show kindness to someone else right now or What will you do to show your generosity towards others?

_____

_____

_____

_____

_____

_____

_____

_____

_____

_____

Disgust Or Hatred – not at all a good karma. Practice empathy.

Humans are clever about repugnant behaviour, and you might feel consumed and trapped by it. Seek out a slight breather by writing about the times you've made other people happy and joyous. Write about jokes you told, or doors have held open by talking, or long extended phone calls you have made to show that you are present? Write about how reassuring another person made you feel. Can you do it again?

Guilt – Right or Wrong?

___

___

___

___

Depression Or Melancholy – raise your voice, talk about it, take action.

Journaling can help you self-soothe through your doubts about depression, but it's not a cure. If you're depressed at an extend which is hampering your physical health too, then go check with a therapist. It is no harm. Also please know that you are not alone and reach out to right person if you can. Meeting with a therapist can provide you with more dedicated prompts for consideration. Same as with anxiety and any mental health concern, there's no shame in seeking support. Write it down about what you feel depressed and why?

___

___

Guilt – Right or Wrong?

Guilt – Right or Wrong?

"Reality finds me sitting sleepily in a polyester robe, writing nonsense into spiral-bound notebooks until my coffee kicks in."

Author's Suggestions To Reconcile Your Guilt

Let's see some quick suggestions on how to cope up and get rid of guilt. If the exercise makes you feel that you are guilt-prone and you tend to fall into the trap of shame and embarrassment which leads you to stress, then these suggestions would help you to live a happy life.

1. Face the feelings of guilt. Release feelings of guilt by speaking about them, sharing, confessing, getting honest about them.

2. Learn to forgive yourself. – Do you judge yourself too bleakly? If yes, then STOP.

3. Scrutinize the origins of your guilt – Is the reason that you feel guilt lucid and reasonable? Check this before entering into guilt. Incongruous or irrational guilt comprise feeling guilty about something that in reality you had little or nothing to do with.

Guilt – Right or Wrong?

4. Change the related or associated behaviour so that the action or actions initiating feelings of guilt and remorse could cease. Simply put: If something you are doing is causing you to feel guilty, then stop doing it and you will no longer have a reason to feel guilty anymore.

5. Elucidate new values for yourself and take real action in the present day instead of dwelling on the past. Think about optimistic action you can take in your life now to feel better. What can you do to improve? Or things going forward?

6. Practice forgiving others, serving others and doing good for others. Be compassionate, learn empathy, this will help you to forgive yourself.

7. Apologize or just seek peace. Is there something you can say or do to try to show that you are willing to make peace with the situation, where there has been pain, conflict, or disagreement?

8. Let go – Let it go the past, so at some point, even if there are things you have done to hurt others and if you are regretful now, you need to let them go. Or, if you are truthfully apologetic over something you

have done wrong in the past and you tried to make peace or amends, you can still forgive yourself even when others do not forgive you.

9. Was there a sincere cause for your past actions that were beyond your control at the time? For example, perhaps you miffed others while you were undergoing untreated mental illness or as the result of active drug or alcohol addiction that you are now making efforts to properly care for. If your deeds were influenced by substance abuse and/or untreated mental health issues, then you should give yourself some sagging about adjudicating yourself too harshly about whatever you might have done when you were not well. Instead, now, focus on real behaviour change which will stimulate better decisions in the present and future.

10. Avoid Shame – (practice journal and worksheets given above in this book – Recommend you to bookmark it).

Guilt – Right or Wrong?

Heal your inner being! I leave you here for a joyful.

Here's a prompt that explores hopefulness and healing: imagine you wake up one day and all your problems are solved. Write about how you'll feel on that day and what you'll do. Invite the celebration.

_____

_____

_____

_____

_____

_____

_____

_____

_____

_____

About Author

Contemporary Indian female poet and winner of several author awards, Shivi Goyal is stimulating and quizzical about the norms in society and spreading love by her chartbuster books that are ruling national and international marketplaces. She is a multi-faceted life, who is an inspiration to the millennials. She is the author of two individual books (Check her books: Words Unsaid... & Love vs= Weed on Amazon.) and 6 anthologies in her kitty. Additionally, she is well known as Author on Travel and taking travel enthusiasts to unknown places with her blogs at www.spiritedblogger.com and other social media platforms.

Proud Guinness Book of World Record Holder and a fabulous human being. She is a proud single mom, who takes life through her meditative lens and writings. She romances with her poems and short stories that lead us to think and question widespread societal taboos. Her writings are motivational and bring healing attitude towards life. You can support her venture Mystopedia Creations by ordering artwork, and books, in turn she dedicates, a certain share to the NGOs for kids and women working for education and their wellbeing. Shivi, firmly believes, that love wins and takes over all the odds in the end.

Connect with her:

Blog - www.spiritedblogger.com

Facebook @spiritedblogger

Instagram @authorontravel

Instagram @mystopedia_creations

YouTube @spiritedblogger

Goodreads @shivigoyal

Read More by the Author

Words Unsaid…   *Love vs= Weed*

Anthologies to read by her as co-author:

- 100 Female Musings
- Chasing Hope
- Khawaish Likhane Ki
- Benevolence
- Aadarshini
- 100 splendid voices by women

Citations

https://osf.io/g389s/

Research Center for Group Dynamics, Institute for Social Research, University of Michigan, Ann Arbor, USA

Psychology Department, Utrecht University, Utrecht, The Netherlands

Developmental Psychology, Leiden University, Leiden, The Netherlands

Dutch Foundation for the Deaf and Hard of Hearing Child, Amsterdam, The Netherlands

https://www.rtor.org/2019/04/29/the-art-of-self-forgiveness/

https://www.oprahdaily.com/life/a26028888/

https://www.heysigmund.com/toxic-people-when-someone-you-love-toxic/

(ref - Fischer, K. W., Shaver, P. R., & Carnochan, P. (1990). How emotions develop and how they organise development. Cognition And Emotion, 4(2), 81-127. doi:10.1080/02699939008407414)

Guilt – Right or Wrong?

Printed in Poland
by Amazon Fulfillment
Poland Sp. z o.o., Wrocław